To Be a Teacher

CORWIN
PRESS

The Corwin Press logo—a raven striding across an open book—represents the happy union of courage and learning. We are a professional-level publisher of books and journals for K-12 educators, and we are committed to creating and providing resources that embody these qualities. Corwin's motto is "Success for All Learners."

To Be a Teacher

Voices From
the Classroom

**Eric Henry
Jeff Huntley
Corinne McKamey
Laura Harper**

CORWIN PRESS, INC.
A Sage Publications Company
Thousand Oaks, California

For information address:

Corwin Press, Inc.
A Sage Publications Company
2455 Teller Road
Thousand Oaks, California 91320

SAGE Publications Ltd.
6 Bonhill Street
London EC2A 4PU
United Kingdom

SAGE Publications India Pvt. Ltd.
M-32 Market
Greater Kailash I
New Delhi 110 048 India

Printed in the United States of America

Library of Congress Cataloging-in-Publication Data

Main entry under title:

To be a teacher: Voices from the classroom / Eric Henry . . . [et al.].
   p.   cm.
  Includes bibliographical references.
  ISBN 0-8039-6323-8 (alk. paper). — ISBN 0-8039-6324-6 (pbk. :
alk. paper)
   1. Student teachers—United States—Biography. 2. Student
teaching—United States. I. Henry, Eric, 1969- .
LB2157.U5T6 1995
370'.7'330973—dc20   95-7734

This book is printed on acid-free paper.

95 96 97 98 99 10 9 8 7 6 5 4 3 2 1

Corwin Press Production Editor: Diane S. Foster
Corwin Press Typesetter: Andrea D. Swanson

Contents

Foreword

Now that you have *To Be a Teacher* in hand, be prepared to experience an explosion of thoughts. And be prepared to experience your full range of emotions. Writing personally, richly, thoughtfully, and compellingly, the authors tell the story of their first experiences as real teachers—a story of rage and hope, of frustration and ecstasy, of bewilderment and insight, of discouragement and inspiration. But most of all, this is a story of personal and professional growth, and a story of love for teaching.

The setting is Mark Twain Middle School, one of four "professional development schools" allied with the 5-year teacher education program at Trinity University in San Antonio, Texas. The voices are those of interns teaching full time during the program's final clinical year. Like most Trinity students, the voices are very white, very bright, and very middle class.

Eric Henry, Laura Harper, and Jeff Huntley completed their undergraduate programs at Trinity University with majors in history and English. They received their bachelor's degrees on Saturday, May 8, 1993. The following Monday they began an intensive fifth-year M.A.T. program by taking a full complement of courses during the summer. Corinne McKamey flew in 2 weeks later, the same day she graduated from Cornell University. In the fall, one week before school opened, they reported to Mark Twain Middle School. Each was an intern assigned to a mentor teacher. They remained a part of the teaching faculty of this school for the full year. Their clinical experiences were complemented by a handful of courses and seminars taught by Trinity faculty, and by mentors from Mark Twain and the other professional development schools.

As part of the graduation requirements, each intern was to compile and present to the faculty and other interns a cumulative portfolio portraying the year's experiences. Portfolios were to speak compellingly to both the personal meanings that the year held for each intern and the intern's readiness to graduate and be licensed as a teacher. Eric, Jeff, Corinne, and Laura decided to use the medium of storytelling to anchor their portfolios. The result was this book, a book of voices.

As a medium, these voices have a Rorschach quality. For each reader, the stories will reveal different images and messages. For each reader, the stories will teach different lessons. One lesson for me was to be reminded that if you want to understand teaching, students, classroom life, and schools, you have to experience them from the inside. Though theories of teaching, adolescence, and schooling fill the pages of textbooks and research journals, they often fail to ring true because of their "de-contextualized" nature. There is a place, of course, for research from a distance, and for thoughtful commentaries on issues of teaching and learning. They can provide needed perspectives without the distractions of the texture and temper of day-by-day living in schools. But for this kind of research and theorizing to account for the problems of practice, and to affect the lives of teachers and children, its revelations must be unpacked and understood from the perspective of the inside life of schools.

Another lesson for me was the ambivalence that I, as a teacher-educator, felt about the issue of cultural diversity, the seam for nearly all of these stories. Let's face it: Most teachers and most students preparing to be teachers are Anglo and monolingual. By contrast, students in states such as Texas and California, and students in most of our urban centers, represent a different population—a population of color and with different cultural identities. I am haunted by this fact. *To Be a Teacher* points to the need for us to do a better job of helping our students view cultural diversity as a resource worth capitalizing on rather than a problem. But how do we communicate this message convincingly to our students?

To varying degrees these four teachers were "blown away" by the shock of differences that they experienced in the students that they were to teach and serve. It wasn't easy, as explained here, for Eric, Jeff, Corinne, and Laura to reach the conclusion that diversity was indeed a resource and not a problem. Happily, they did. What did it take? Two things, I think. First, it took a sense of being called to serve—to view teaching as an "addiction" to use Eric's word. Second, it took being immersed in the problems of practice from the very beginning of the fifth year. Sure, cultural diversity topics were covered in the courses that preceded the clinical year, but one doesn't change one's views about cultural matters so much by taking courses or by reading books. The proof is in the experience.

In the end, *To Be a Teacher* is about the personal struggle of four novice teachers to become the kinds of teachers they want to be. Part of this struggle involves coming to know oneself—one's strengths and weaknesses, values and beliefs, and knowledge and skills. It involves being able to use this knowledge of self to make good decisions about teaching, learning, and student development.

Coming to know oneself and learning to use this self-knowledge productively is tough enough even under the best of conditions. But why do we seem to make it so hard? We organize schools, for example, and we engage in the rituals of schooling that this organization requires, in ways that encourage the distancing and hardening of student subcultures. Why are student norms so strong and so overpowering? Why is it so hard to domesticate these norms? It is common among progressive educators to point out that you have to know students well in order to teach them well. But why do we organize for schooling and think about teaching and learning in ways that make this knowing so hard to achieve?

These questions belie simple answers. But *To Be a Teacher* suggests to me that part of the problem is our *gesellschaft* theories of schooling. Ferdinand Tonnies (1957) distinguishes between two theories of society that are represented in two ideal types of social organizations. In *gemeinschaft*, relationships among people are valued as ends in themselves. People are connected to each other because they share similar values, ideas, and ideals. These communal commitments create strong and unifying norms that compel people to behave in certain ways. *Gesellschaft* organizations, on the other hand, are characterized by impersonal, mechanistic, and instrumental relationships and behavior. Behavior in *gesellschaft* organizations is governed less by shared ideas and ideals and more by individual calculations of self-interest.

Gemeinschaft translates to community. Though we often use the term *learning community* to describe schools, underneath they remain largely *gesellschaft* in their fundamental character. But suppose the students at Mark Twain began their school careers in kindergarten and continued throughout the grades in schools that were true communities. Would there be a difference in what these four interns experienced at Mark Twain? I think so. In communities, for example, the connection of people to purposes and the connections between people are based not on contracts, deals, and other manifestations of self-interest but on commitments. Communities are socially organized around relationships and the felt interdependencies that nurture them. Communities, too, are confronted with issues of control. But instead of relying on external control measures, communities rely more on norms and values. Once established, the ties of community in schools can become substitutes for the various organizational schemes, disciplined management plans, and other structural devices that seek to influence what students and teachers believe and do.

The paradox in all of this is that the need to experience *gemein-schaft* is part of our human nature. Young people in particular have this need. If they can't find *gemeinschaft* in the official life of the school, they create "community" amongst themselves. Too often these student subcultures work against the purposes of schools and the aspirations of teachers, no matter how noble they might be. *To Be a Teacher* beams with the determination of these interns to penetrate, to reach in and touch, to bring students out and a little bit closer, and to create community anew. My prayer is that they will not give up over time.

The lessons I gleaned from *To Be a Teacher* are mine. Yours will be yours. But one lesson that I think most of us will learn is that teaching is a moral activity. Eric, Jeff, Corinne, and Laura care, and caring counts. For them, teaching is a form of pedagogy.

> The original Greek idea of pedagogy had associated with it the meaning of leading in the sense of accompanying the child and living with the child in such a way as to provide direction and care for his or her life. (van Manen, 1991, p. 38)

Teachers have the opportunity to practice a form of pedagogical leadership because they stand foremost and closest in a caring relationship to children. They have the major responsibility for guiding young people academically, socially, and spiritually through the world of childhood to adulthood. The process of education itself implies engaging in a kind of moral leadership. Young people, as van Manen explains, must eventually grow out of (*educere*, which means to lead out of) the world of childhood, and adults must help children grow into (*educare*, which means to lead into) the world of adulthood. The message of *To Be a Teacher* is that whatever else teaching might be, at its root it is a form of moral leadership.

Thomas J. Sergiovanni

References

Tonnies, F. (1957). *Community and society* (C. P. Loomis, Ed. and Trans.) New York: HarperCollins.

van Manen, M. (1991). *The tact of teaching: The meaning of pedagogical thoughtfulness.* Albany: State University of New York Press.

Prologue

The scene: Two years later, a trio of young teachers converge upon a familiar meeting place, a diner in the heart of San Antonio, Texas. They smile at each other as they emerge from their automobiles and, without need for words, go inside. They follow the instructions, "Seat Yourself," and find a round, extra-large booth capable of holding the stacks of paper and laptop computers they have brought with them. Coffees are ordered all around; it will be a long Saturday afternoon.

Jeff: Glad you could drive down, Laura. It's almost as if we never graduated.

Laura: This does seem familiar, doesn't it?

Corinne: Except that Eric's teaching down in Guatemala.

Laura: Have you heard from him?

Corinne: I sent the news of our pending publication, so we probably won't hear for a few weeks.

Laura: Up in Austin, I feel as if I have this different life now. When I come down here, it's like returning to a dream or from a dream— I can't decide which.

Laura's eyes drop to the Xeroxed stack in front of her. She opens the manila manuscript folder and begins to read. . . .

Silence is a rare noise at Mark Twain Middle School. Teachers' and students' voices compete to fill the school with their stories. Many become lost in the chaos or become decaying jumbles of personalities and anecdotes that slowly fade from memory.

When we were intern teachers at Twain, we struggled with our assignment: To create a portfolio of artifacts, personal observations, and philosophy that would demonstrate what we learned during our intern year. We chose instead to compile our experiences as a collection of stories. The stories served not only as personal diaries but also as a demonstration of professional reflection—a key component of our teacher education program.

In our continuing education as teachers, we want these stories not only to remind us where we have come from but, more important, to teach us something with each reading. Our hope is that others will read our stories and learn something as well. The voices echoing from our rooms contain the raw confusion, ambiguity, fits and bursts of disappointment, laughter, anger, and satisfaction that have taught us to be teachers. We hope that the chorus of voices that have helped shape our intern experiences at Mark Twain Middle School will keep alive one of the most challenging and exciting years we may ever have.

Mark Twain is an urban middle school with a large population of at-risk students. The many challenges the school provides are no match for the supportive minds and spirits that inhabit its halls. The faculty and staff has committed itself to multidisciplinary, alternative curricula in a quest for higher academic standards and a richer education for the students. The creative minds of Twain were perhaps the spark that enabled us to see a different paradigm for expressing our learning as interns there.

And, of course, the students were undoubtedly the inspiration. Oh, in the beginning they may have had another name, such as "the affliction that caused our psychosis." But after entering our storytelling full-swing, we recognized our work as the product of our struggle and not merely as a coping strategy. As you will see, we believed that their voices were as much a part of our teaching soul as our own. We have not forgotten to listen.

We also give credit to Trinity University for setting us to the task of thinking about our role as teachers. Perhaps we thought too much; all our professors wanted was a voluminous portfolio of sights, sounds, and experiences from our year, and some carefully crafted reflections. Through our thinking we scared ourselves into a frenzy of creative activity and had neither time nor courage to look back from it. We ended up where we were through a bit of prodding; a bit of chance; a lot of wondering, hoping, moping, crying, and laughing; glimmers of temporary insanity; and endless support.

We must conclude by naming the following people whose belief in our abilities as teachers and skills as writers has sustained us to this point: our Mark Twain mentor teachers Benita Longoria, Sylvia Lovelace, Patsy Richards, Evelyn Sanders, and Geoffrey Stirrup; our Trinity teachers, professors John Moore and Thomas Sergiovanni; our parents; and the rest of the Third Cohort of Interns at Mark Twain Middle School, Jeanette Donahue, Jennifer McCready, Kathleen McGurk, Heather Russel, and Shannon Walsh.

"The bell has rung! Please take your seats. And by all means, listen up!"

About the Authors

Laura Harper teaches reading and writing at Georgetown Junior High School, Georgetown, Texas. She received a B.A. in English and history and an M.A.T. in secondary education from Trinity University, San Antonio, Texas.

Eric Henry teaches secondary social studies at the Inter-American School in Quetzaltenango, Guatemala. He graduated from Trinity University with a B.A. in composite social studies and an M.A.T. in secondary education.

Jeff Huntley teaches sixth-, seventh-, and eighth-grade reading at the Southwest Enrichment Center, San Antonio, Texas. He graduated cum laude from Trinity University, San Antonio, Texas, with a B.A. in English and an M.A.T. in secondary education.

Corinne McKamey teaches sixth-, seventh-, and eighth-grade science at the Southwest Enrichment Center, San Antonio, Texas. She graduated from Cornell University with a B.S. in biology and society and received an M.A.T. in secondary education from Trinity University, San Antonio, Texas.

Thomas J. Sergiovanni is the Lillian Radford Professor of Education and Administration at Trinity University in San Antonio, Texas, where he teaches in the school leadership and the teacher education program.

ONE

Ms. McKamey

*"To understand teaching you have to be there,
engrossed in the human interactions."*

On the Outside Looking In

"What do you mean you don't have a textbook?" Dr. Holtz looked at my mentor, Patsy, and me in disbelief.

"We don't have a book," Patsy answered, "I mean, we do have a book: a life science textbook. But that isn't what we are teaching, so we don't use it much. You see, we are piloting the Science I curriculum, which integrates *all* sciences: life, earth, and physical sciences, as well as chemistry and physics. . . ."

"So what kind of curriculum do you use?" Dr. Holtz interrupted.

"We use what we need," Patsy said.

"But where do you get it?" Dr. Holtz began rapping his pencil on the desk.

"Books, folders, the library, other teachers . . . I don't know. . . . different places," I said.

"And how do you know what you are going to teach?"

I looked at Patsy. "Where's our planning book?"

"It's right here," she answered. "We sat down at the beginning of the year and outlined what we wanted to cover and in what order," she said.

"We started with rules and safety, then went in order: scientific method, chemistry, states of matter, rocks and minerals, energy, geological processes, planets, oceans. . . . It served as a basis for what we wanted to do. When we got lost, we referred back to our outline. It's been very handy."

"I see," Dr. Holtz answered.

"Not being tied to a book gives us flexibility," I continued. "Next week we are going on a field trip to Enchanted Rock State Park as an outgrowth of our initial unit on rocks and minerals."

Holtz changed the subject. "So which classes do you teach, Corinne?"

I looked at Patsy. There really wasn't a straight answer to that one either. Most Trinity interns had chosen two or three classes to teach consistently. My schedule wasn't so easy to define.

"Well," I began, "I teach all of the classes some of the time, and sometimes Patsy and I team teach."

Holtz kept looking at me expectantly. He wasn't completely satisfied with my answer.

"It depends on the day and the lesson," I continued. "For instance, I taught a lot of the energy unit during the past 6 weeks. Patsy has been teaching more lately because she is more knowledgeable about geology. Sometimes we teach all day. Often, though, we take notes during the other's lesson and use it to teach succeeding classes. By seventh period, we have vastly improved our lesson."

"Seventh period is a different story," Patsy countered my statement. She looked at me. "Does he know about seventh period?"

I looked at Dr. Holtz. "Seventh period?" he asked.

"Several students in seventh period could not handle a regular classroom setting, so we have divided the class into two groups. One uses an interactive curriculum and the other a separate, very book-oriented, structured curriculum. It takes both of us to teach that period."

"I see," Dr. Holtz answered.

But did he see? Sometimes even I didn't understand my classroom.

Every time I tried to explain my classroom to anyone— the true classroom, the kids, the experiences, the discipline—I found it difficult to capture it in words.

You couldn't really understand my classroom unless you were there: engrossed in a lesson or an activity, knew the kids, and understood the context of school within their lives.

I could give you the nonliving artifacts of my classroom: lesson plans, seating charts, and grade book. I could give you parts of my students: essays and tests, pictures of projects, and accounts of cooperative learning activities. You might then have an idea about what kind of classroom I have.

It isn't the same as being there.

If you were to flip through some of my students' work, you might notice that Raymond Arias got a 100% on a test about food webs. You wouldn't know what a feat it was to get Raymond to even turn in a test.

By not being there, you miss out on the best part of teaching—the human interactions.

When I call my parents, siblings, or friends from college, I tell them stories about my classroom. I want them to know why these kids are so important to me and why teaching gives me so many headaches and satisfactions. Stories are the next best thing to being there.

Siberia

※

The question usually comes out in the same tone of voice as "You are going on a vacation to Siberia? Oh."

"You will be interning at Mark Twain next year? Oh."

Most middle school teachers get similar remarks with accompanying condolences and looks of pity. Mark Twain, an inner-city middle school, merited extra frosting on the cake. Kids from this school were from broken homes, were in gangs, carried guns, and who knows what else. I remember I had a discussion with my mother that summer; she wasn't exactly thrilled with the prospect of my teaching at Twain. "Why don't you ask to be placed somewhere else?" she asked. "Are you sure about what you are getting yourself into?" I wasn't.

Most students in the program with me had done some undergraduate work at Mark Twain; I transferred into the graduate program from a university back East and could only make dubious inferences from the grievances I heard. I wasn't quite sure what to expect.

I went down to Twain one afternoon to see for myself. . . .

There are a few characteristics intrinsic to every middle school. Walking into the school reminded me of them. The smell: a blend of musty and new textbooks, biology formaldehyde, and a cafeteria odor that smells of burnt plastic and overstewed gym socks. The colors: Green #36 and Pink #204, industrial colors that also appear frequently in public restrooms and hospitals. The look: long, outstretched hallways, with rows of graffitied lockers and scattered bulletin boards. The sound: echoing rumbles of laughter and shouts, lockers slamming, sneakers squeaking. Even in an empty building, these sounds still lurk in the corners of the hallways; it would not be a school without them.

I thought back to a *Newsweek* article I had read a month earlier. Some inner-city schools, the article had said, had changed from social, nurturing centers of learning to metal-detected, high-security daily holding pens. I scanned the hallway searching for some menacing, out-of-control students, but I saw only a few normal-looking students on purposeful missions to the bathrooms, to the library, or with messages for other teachers. I looked around for a metal detector or even the inevitable hall monitor checking for passes—there were none. Where was the tight security? Where were the uncontrollable heathens?

I went outside to the portable classrooms. Three boys were sitting with their backs to the schoolyard fence. I saw another jump out a classroom doorway to join them. Closest to me sat a small boy, arms folded and toe scraping the ground.

"What are you all doing out here?" I asked.

"It's the substitute, man. She threw us out of the classroom." I looked at my watch; there were still 30 minutes left in the period. Beyond the torn hurricane fence he was using as a backrest, the freedom of a schoolless day beckoned.

"Why haven't you left? What is keeping you around school?" I asked.

"Where would I go?" The boy looked up from his shoe, and then his eyes nervously trailed back to the ground. "All I asked for was a pencil," he mumbled to himself.

A bolder boy approached me.

"Are you a new teacher?"

"I will be next year—in the Eagles."

"That's what I'll be next year," he said excitedly.

"Well then, I'll be one of your science teachers," I answered.

"That's all right!"

All through the conversation I was thinking to myself, what did these boys do to get thrown out of the classroom and how bad can they be? And, are these the kids my mother was worried about? They seemed like just scared, innocent kids to me.

In my first semester of teaching, I found that Twain kids are just that—kids. Some of them are a bit messed up, some are a little misdirected, and a few I wouldn't trust with my back turned. Yet, kids have endearing qualities that grow on you, if you take the time to get to know them.

One day, I spent 30 minutes out in the hall with three of my own students who had been thrown out of the classroom. Each was a gang member. One even admitted to me that he had been in a drive-by shooting a month before and was being pressured to be in another one the next weekend.

"Why do you guys use violence to resolve violence?" I asked. "Aren't you afraid to die?"

"Miss," Noel said, "Three of my brothers have been shot and killed by the Ambrose. My father was shot last week in the arm. They thought he was me. You gonna tell me that I should sit around and wait for them to come around and knock me off? They shot my brothers, man. I owe them. A B-boy sticks up for his brothers, man. If I die, I die a Blue Boy." I listened in silence. He looked up at me. "TTTh, You're a white college girl; what do you know about my life? You wouldn't understand." I looked at Noel.

"You're right," I said. "I don't understand."

When Noel left school, he carried a gun. For all I knew, he shot people on the weekends. I still liked him. I still wanted to help him. It frustrates me that kids like Noel have to live in a world where violence is accepted. It frustrates me even more that few of them realize that not everyone lives under the shadow of inner-city violence.

My students watched a film on volcanoes one day. A scene in the movie showed a village being engulfed by a huge lava flow.

"Miss!" Sandra cried incredulously after the film. "Why would anyone want to live next to a volcano? Why didn't they move away?"

"Sandra, there are people in this world who would never live in inner-city San Antonio because of the violence and gang activity. Why does your family stay in San Antonio?" Sandra thought a minute.

Johnny answered the question. "It's our home, Miss. Why would we want to move away?"

My initial fears of Twain kids may have had some truth to them. Some of those students are hard-core kids. What is most frightening is becoming aware of the environment in which some of them live and watching that become manifest in the children themselves. The bottom line is that these kids are still just kids in need of a teacher.

The year has begun to close and I am pretty sure I want to stay in the inner-city schools. Mom, of course, is still not so thrilled. "Why not get a nice job in Alamo Heights?" she asks.

I answer, "But Mom, these are my kids. . . . I am their teacher. Why would I want to teach anywhere else?"

The Adopted

I sat squished in the back of a van with 18 little girls. We were on our way to a nearby nursing home. A hand, palm licked and coated with blue crystals, was thrust into my face. "Here, Miss, you want some Kool Aid powder?" Rosemary's hand lowered and I looked into her questioning eyes. She was testing me. I laughed.

"Off of your licked hand? Do you all share gum too?"

A voice came from behind, "Yeah, Miss. Look!" Maria's hand reached over my shoulder and deposited a bright purple wad onto Rosemary's waiting (and bright blue) tongue. I felt those peer-pressuring eyes on me from all directions. As a teacher, I had a duty to tell them to put the sugar away. But as an after-school program sponsor, my role was less defined.

I licked my palm. "Okay," I said, "But only if you promise that it won't turn my teeth blue."

"It won't, Miss!" They squealed in excitement. So began my relationship with some of my loudest seventh graders.

In class, they had produced more chatter and giggles than completed assignments. Getting them to think about more than boys and gossip had been a challenging, if not impossible, task. Rosemary, for example, had failed four of her seven classes in the previous grading period. I felt a foot in my lap.

"Crystal, sit down! Where are you going?"

"Miss, I have to tell Maria something!"

"Can't you tell her from here?" I looked around the van and noticed other girls were crawling over each other. Don't open a window, I thought, someone will surely get pushed out.

"Everybody sit down! We are almost there." The chatter had risen to a low rumble.

"Okay, Miss!" I heard a few of them shout back.

Was the nursing home ready for us? "What are you all going to do first when we get there?" I asked.

"Oh Miss, why do you keep asking us those questions?" a voice called from behind me. More laughter.

Too late to back out, I thought as the van pulled into the parking lot. We are here.

As the door slid open, the giggles tumbled out of the van and bounced up the ramp to the nursing home door. The carefree glints in their eyes changed to apprehension and shyness, and a sudden quietness gripped the group. No one moved. Faces turned to look at me expectantly. I smiled and answered, "Well, what are you waiting for? Let's go!" One small step and they bounded through the door.

A pool of urine sat like a welcome mat in the middle of the floor. Tables and wheelchairs were scattered carelessly about the room, and the residents sleepily looked up at our spectacle. Oh Lord, I thought, the kids are going to freak out any minute and go running back out that door. I could tell there was a slight hesitation in the group, and then Rosemary stepped over the puddle and walked up to a group of ladies sewing pillows at a nearby table. Kids paired off in twos and threes and infiltrated the room. Why had I been worried?

"Are you their teacher, honey?" a high, raspy voice asked as I felt a tug on my shirt. A gnarled, black hand grasped my hand, and I looked into a pair of eyes magnified by inch-thick glasses.

"I am," I said as I squeezed the lady's hand, "My name is Corinne."

"Co-rinne," the lady pronounced. "Nice to meet you."

"What school are you all from?" she asked.

"Twain Middle School," I answered.

"Mark Twain?" Her voice screeched. Her eyes became very distant as she looked out the window. "I taught school at Twain." She looked back up at me, "But that was many years ago, you understand."

"Yes ma'am," I said. "I bet things have changed a bit since you taught school."

"These young ones don't have any sense any more. No manners, no sense of family. Why, I bet they spend more time in front of the television set than they do with their parents. You know what they learn from the television?" She looked at me.

"What?" I asked.

"Nothin' but violence and sex, that's what. Those shows have them so mixed up that they don't know the difference between right and wrong. The only good influence they got is from school." She squeezed my hand again. "You teach them right, you hear?" She nodded across the room, let go of my hand, and closed her eyes. I followed her nod to see the rest of the room. It had transformed itself into crazy mayhem.

Tejano music flowed from one corner of the room and was accompanied by pounding piano tunes from the other corner. In the middle of it all, Dalia, Garza, and Jose were dancing a polka. Rosemary and Sarah were pushing Mr. Viramontes around the room in circles. Several girls had struck up a game of dominoes with two residents. What wonderful noise!

The hands of the clock moved to 4:20. Time to go. The roaring laughter had peaked and subsided to chatter and an occasional shout across the room.

"Twain people, let's wrap things up, we need to get you all back to school." A few bolted for the door, but most of them ignored me. After circulating twice around the room, I had most of them rounded up and herded back out the door.

"Bye! See you next week!" Rosemary called as she waved. Residents' hands waved in response, and their gaze followed us out the door. The low rumble of excitement, though half gone without the kids, still vibrated throughout the room. "Bye!"

Everyone piled back into the van and I slid the door shut. Silence. I saw sullen faces trapped in thought. I let them reflect. There wasn't a sound for 2 whole minutes until I turned around and asked, "Why's everyone so quiet?" Eyes were looking out the window or down at the floor. There was silence for a moment and then voices came from all directions.

"That isn't a very good place for people to live."

"Those nurses don't care about our adopted grandparents."

"Just look at the dining room we were in—those tables all scattered around and that pee had been there all day."

"Aren't you all being a bit harsh?" I interrupted.

"Miss, I am serious," Rosemary said. "None of those nurses care; one was sitting in a chair in the corner while Mr. Viramontes needed to go back to his room. And Miss Keller had spilled coffee all down her shirt and no one had come to clean her up. They just left her like that. It's terrible! I would never put my parents in a home like that."

"Not all homes are like that," I answered.

"I don't care. No one cares about them; Dalia said that hardly anyone comes to visit her. They are all just sitting around waiting to die. I bet no one would even notice if one of them did."

"You would notice, Rosemary," I answered back. "Don't you think you could make a difference in their lives?" I looked at the sea of faces.

"Did you all notice how happy your grandparents were when we left?" My question was answered by silent disbelief. I continued, "You all brought energy into that place that wasn't there before. Mr. Viramontes was laughing, Margarita was dancing, and that lady by the door talked the whole time we were there." Giggles came from beside me.

"Ms. Garcia wouldn't stop talking. . . . We just asked her one question," Maria said. "She had a lot to say."

"Yeah," Sarah added, "I made the mistake of telling her that I knew a little bit of Spanish and then got trapped! I just kept saying, 'Uh huh' and 'Si' and she kept right on talking."

"She probably doesn't get asked questions very often. I bet you made her day," I said.

"Yeah, I guess we did make her day," Sandy answered. "And we'll be back next week."

Kids started talking again, discussing conversations they had had with their grandparents and planning next week's visit. I sank back into my seat. The old schoolteacher's words still rang in my head: "They have no sense of family. Kids today don't know the difference between right and wrong."

Don't they?

It's Just Different, That's All

"You can sit here," Betsy said as she walked over to a corner desk. Her floppy ears bounced with her step, and her tail gave a little shake. She turned back to me, and she scratched her black nose. "Kids are likely to be a bit wild today seeing it's Halloween. Third period is my loudest class, too, so keep that in mind. They are only ninth graders, not too far off from middle school." Betsy's clear blue eyes shone from underneath her hood. "And if anyone asks," she said, "I am a Koala, not a mouse."

I smiled. "You make a cute Koala."

"Thanks," she said. She grabbed her tail and swung it as she walked back to her desk.

"Let me know if you need anything," Betsy continued. "I need to get set up for class."

"Okay." I slid into the desk and opened my notebook. A cowboy, a witch, two male cheerleaders, and a few students began filtering into the classroom. Despite the festivities, it was eerily quiet.

My own seventh-grade classroom was a very different story.

A blur of curls and the scent of hair spray dashed into the room. "I'm going to get you!" Maria screamed to Janie. She had a can of Aqua Net hairspray held out in front of her. Like a neurotic little dog, a green sweater tugged and tossed behind Janie's left heel. She squealed, "Are not!" and pounced on top of a desk. Before my mouth could open in protest, Josh and Larry, my two largest gorillas, pounded a few giant steps, jumped to dangle from the door frame, and then swung into the middle of the floor. They both looked back and then down at their feet. Larry bent his shoulders down and turned away. "Ahhh, beat by 2 inches," he said.

Josh strutted towards the two screaming girls, "You haven't beat me all week," he said proudly under his breath.

Four had made it to the room—33 students to go. The beginning of class was always a new surprise.

I found that if I yelled consistently for a week, gave lunch detentions, and called parents, I could quell the chaos to a low rumble. Given time restrictions and piles of in-between class paperwork, I had learned to deal with chaos, at least for a while.

Betsy's class, on the other hand, took their seats calmly just in time for the bell to ring.

"Hey Miss Burke, what are you, a mouse?" Some boy in the back asked. Betsy looked up from her roll sheet and pointed to the sentence written on the board: "I am a Koala, not a mouse."

I chuckled.

No teacher shushing, no threats, no constant student squirming, no lofted airplanes.

Although situated on the side of the classroom, I sat beside a girl, and behind me was a pair of boys sporting cheerleader skirts and baseball caps. The girl whispered to me, "Are you new?"

"Uh huh," I said as I nodded my head. I hadn't thought of what the students would think of me. Donning my usual jeans and sweater and having my hair pulled back in a headband, I looked more like a student than a teacher. My attention turned back to Betsy at the front of the class.

"Let's go over some of your homework problems," she said. "How many of you weren't here yesterday?"

I raised my hand. She came by, winked, and gave me a Xerox copy of some genetic problems.

"Okay," she continued. "Which ones did you have problems with?"

I settled back, enjoying my review of dihybrid crosses. The girl beside me was slow to take notes, and I let her look over my right shoulder as I scribbled out the problems. I looked around at the class.

Everyone, with the exception of one of the cheerleaders behind me, was engrossed in the lesson. The boy sat and tapped his pencil and cracked jokes periodically. No one took notice of him.

Studious faces. Patience. Diligence. Concentration. The ideals middle school teachers strive to attain in their students.

In middle school, I had become quite adept in educational espionage. I slipped curriculum into class like a mother hides vitamins in a kid's dessert. Students were like every other kid who preferred the brightly colored, sugarcoated cereals that come with prizes to more wholesome cereals with more substantive nutrients.

"It's good for us?" They would look at me in horror. "Yuck!"

As the year progressed, I had begun to slowly intersperse games laced with curriculum with lessons that reeked of knowledge. Some were beginning to get a taste for it. Most left it on their desks or the blackboard or hanging in the air, rejected and undigested. "Yuck!"

Betsy's voice carried into my thoughts. "This problem is a bit hard to imagine on paper. I've got some chromosomes with these genes already linked on them. . . ." Betsy started placing magnetized pipe cleaners on the board. Chromosomes met in the middle of the blackboard, paired off, and separated.

"Do you see how chance comes into play here?"

The girl beside me, still confused, raised her hand.

"Natalie?" Betsy asked.

"Could you do that problem one more time? I still don't get it." A few heads nodded in agreement. Others who were caught up turned to figuring out the next problem.

Here was the difference. Middle school teaching usually worked in an MTV-type format: something new and different every few minutes. High school was a feature-length movie with few intermissions.

The bell rang. "Okay, class, try to finish these problems tonight and we will go on to linked genes tomorrow," Betsy said as she walked over to my desk. "What'd you think?"

"High school is a whole new world. My seventh graders would never sit through a class like that."

As I spoke, the cheerleader passed behind me. "Hey!" He interrupted. "You mean you aren't a new student?"

I felt a bit like a traitor.

"No, I am in Ms. Burke's class at Trinity. I was here to see what high school is like."

The boy walked toward the door and called to the girl who had sat beside me, "Did you know that that girl is one of Ms. Burke's friends from Trinity?"

As I left the high school, I passed ghouls, goblins, and more male cheerleaders, and a few girls glittered from head to toe. They walked a bit fast; the high school was big and some had to hike to make it before the bell. I wondered what kind of kids were behind those masks. I looked hard, but only noticed a few characters out of the crowd.

I drove to the middle school to finish out the day. As I walked through the hallway, raw emotions bounced off the lockers and echoed off the floors. I could see into every kid's eyes, into every kid's mind. As I rounded the corner to the room, my third-period students clustered around me.

"Where were you, Miss?" the circle asked.

"I was at the high school observing a biology class."

"The high school?" I again felt like a traitor.

"Yes, the high school," I answered.

Two boys darted down the hall in a heated game of chase.

"Slow down!" I yelled.

"But Miss, he's got my pencil!" Carlos called over his shoulder as he continued running after the other boy.

Down the hall, a girl kicked a locker in a spark of anger. Laughter spilled out of the classroom door beside me.

My circle of third period remained around me.

"Did you like high school better?" Christy asked me.

I put my arm around her. "High school is just different, that's all."

She put her arm around my waist. "I'm glad you are back."

"Me too," I said.

Marvin

Ms. Garza, the speech therapist, had a hunch.

"Marvin, do you know the days of the week?" Marvin looked at his speech teacher; his stray eye wandered to the corner of the room.

"Yes." He folded his arms and lowered his head.

"Can you tell them to me?"

Marvin's good eye looked at his hands as he counted on his fingers: "Tuesday, Sunday, Saturday, Monday, Wednesday, and. . . ." He recounted on his fingers, " . . . Friday."

Leaning forward, the speech teacher placed her hands on Marvin's knees. "Can you tell them to me in order?"

"In what order?" Marvin pulled back suddenly.

"In the order that they happen every week," the teacher answered.

Both of Marvin's eyes now roved the room. There was a confused silence.

Ms. Garza paused after telling her story to me. "He can't tell you the months of the year in order, either."

"How did he get to the seventh grade?" I murmured to myself.

Ms. Garza continued her train of thought: "I am supposed to be helping him to refine his expressions, but if he doesn't remember that Tuesday, the day we meet, is on the day after Monday, what good am I doing? I have to start at the beginning."

Marvin could sequence some events. I thought back to the earthworm dissection. Marvin had tutored Martha, a gifted student, on lab procedures. His main thrust had been the importance of sequencing the dissection steps.

Marvin functioned best if he knew that his knowledge could be useful, especially if he was needed by other people like Martha or a team. Despite Marvin's showing flashes of his abilities, most people did not expect much in the way of responses from him. But I began to notice his abilities during a review game I did for a test.

"What's the score, Miss?"

I counted the points up. "We are currently tied, ladies and gentlemen. This last question will determine the winner. Raise your hand and I'll call on you if you've answered less than twice." Hector's brow wrinkled.

"Can we help out our teammates?" I could tell what Hector was thinking: Everyone on his team had answered two or three questions except for Marvin. Both Hector and I turned our attention to the corner of the room where Marvin sat drawing a picture of Mickey Mouse on a scrap of wrinkled up paper.

I looked down at Hector and lowered my voice, "Nope," I said. Hector, and the rest of his teammates who understood the implications of my statement, slumped their shoulders. Jeannette, behind Marvin, poked him into attention. "You're up, Marvin. Better listen to this next question," she whispered.

I projected my voice so that the whole class would hear me. "We have already said water and sunlight. What is the third component of photosynthesis?" I asked. Isabel, on Team II, raised her hand first.

"Isabel?"

"Oxygen?" The minute her answer hit the air Isabel's side of the room moaned discordantly. Team I's hands and voices sprang into action: "Me, Miss, pick me!" The loudest was Marvin, of all people.

"Marvin?" I called. Team I countermoaned.

Hector threw his pencil down. "That's it, that's the game. We've lost for sure." At the same time, Team II's faces brightened. They now had a probable chance at recovering from their mistake.

"I know it I know it I know it!" Marvin's excitement burst through his arms and he sprang to his feet.

"What is the last component of photosynthesis, Marvin?" I encouraged.

Marvin froze, leg propped on a chair, torso twisted toward me. His hands were clenched, and his eyes, usually straying to different areas of the room, focused on the corner of a desk in front of me. He looked up, his face skewed in frustration. His mouth opened, as if testing the air, and then closed again.

"It . . . I.I . . . IT is C . . . CC . . . CCC," Marvin's greedy brain was trying its darndest to hang onto the words. The phrase vibrated and then dropped from his mouth like a raindrop, "CCC . . . Carbon DDD . . . Dioxssiiide."

Astonishment.

The room was silent.

"Carbon dioxide!" I said. "Right! Team I wins!"

Team I students hollered in excitement, "Marvin! You did it!"

As he slid back into his chair, Marvin's smile radiated throughout the room. He focused both eyes on me for a moment, scanned the room, and then mouthed the words, "I did it!"

Camping Lessons

"... Nah, a cat with diarrhea is the worst: It shoots out in a stream...."

"Think about cows! They have four stomachs. That's extra ammunition." The kids' voices trailed up to the driver's seat from the back of the van. I had to laugh.

"What are you all talking about back there?"

"Miss!" John called in a serious tone. "We are trying to figure out which animal has the worst diarrhea!"

I laughed again. I had forgotten what it was like to be 12. Even though I taught them science all day, teaching 12-year-olds was much different than thinking like them. There are many things that I took for granted that these kids—Jose, Robert, Violet, Humberto, Lindy, John, Veronica, and others— were yet to learn....

Lesson 1: How Far Depends On When You Get There

"How much longer, Miss?"

"We haven't even gotten out of San Antonio yet, guys!"

"Well, how much longer?"

"At least an hour."

"Wow! We are really going far!"

The engine coughed at the mention of a long distance. CLANK! Pock-pock-pock, CLANK! Pock-pock-pock.

I tried to ignore it. I looked over at Jose. "It's nothing serious, do you think?"

"Nah, just bad gas, Miss."

As if clearing its throat, the engine coughed louder.

CLANK! POCK-POCK-POCK.

And then it settled down to a low grumble.

Two minutes out of Bandera, it had an emphysema attack. CLANK-POCK-POCK-CLANK-CLANK-CLANK-POCK-CLANK...!

As we topped a hill, I could see the Dairy Queen sign sprouting up out of an asphalt parking lot. The engine quit, and we began to roll, and roll, and roll. We reached the parking lot, and then nothing.

As I climbed out of the van, Laura Harper called from the window of her car, "Glad y'all made it!"

"Yeah, well," I gave a laugh, "just barely. We're gonna be here a while. The van is dead."

"You mean we are stuck here in a PARKING LOT?" Josh asked.

"Well, we are only 12 miles from our camping spot."

"But we ARE HERE, in a PARKING LOT!"

Mr. Henry pulled out a hacky sack from his pocket. "Do you all know the fine arts of granola games?" he asked.

Lesson 2: Basic Necessities

"I have to use the restroom," Violet said to me, her arms twisting the bottom of her shirt. Several other girls had heard the gist of the conversation and drew closer.

I stood up, dinner bags in hand.

"Well, the girls' tree is that way," I said, pointing to a cove of trees lurking to the right of our camp.

Violet peered into the darkness, looked back down at the tail of her shirt, and said, "I can hold it." As she turned away, the other girls' shoulders slumped, and Lindy's legs crossed.

Ms. Harper dropped her pack and announced, "Okay, any girls who want to learn how to pee in the woods, follow me." Seven girls dropped what they were doing and followed Laura to the trees. I looked back down at dinner. I had five bags. There were supposed to be six. One can of tuna, a box of raisins, and the most important dinner utensil, the can opener, were still tucked away in someone's pack.

Ms. Harper's voice rang clear into camp, "You have to pull your pants down here, past your knees...." The three boys snickered.

"These are the important things in camping," I said to them. I returned to my organizing.

"What's for dinner?" Humberto asked.

"What time did Domino's say they'd be here with the pizzas?" asked Mr. Henry.

"Domino's?" asked Humberto.

"You mean you forgot to call Domino's from the Dairy Queen in Bandera?"

Humberto cracked a smile, "Nah, Miss, we're having tuna; I saw it in one of the dinner bags."

Dinner was fine cuisine.

"Eeew! You mean we are eating TUNA FISH and RANCH DRESSING!"

"It's Tuna NuNu," said Ms. Harper. "You squish it around in your Ziplock bag and then squeeze it out onto your English muffin."

The kids scrunched up their noses and then someone said, "Someone pass me the ranch dressing. . . ."

Lesson 3: "Don't Get Hysterical."

"Miss, Miss, Miss, Miss!" Lindy whispered as she crawled over my head and tugged at the zipper of the tent door. I opened my eyes. "Miss, I have to go, I really have to. . . . I can't wait, please, Miss, help me get out. . . ."

I sat up and drowsily said, "Lindy, calm down, getting hysterical is only going to make things worse." Lindy's eyes were almost yellow and she bounced up and down on her knees. The first thought that hit me was, I hope she doesn't pee on her rented sleeping bag. I looked over; she was sitting on the floor of the tent.

"Miss, you've got to open it. I've got to go!"

I twisted my body over to the door and began pulling on the zipper. It was caught in a dozen folds of fabric.

"Just a sec, Lindy, it's . . ."

"Miss, I can't wait, I can't wait, I have to . . ."

Silence.

I looked over my shoulder. Lindy had stopped bouncing.

"Miss, I did it."

Lesson 4: Bandannas Can Be Lifesavers

We sat in our circle of 16, and Ms. Harper pulled out a wad of bandannas from her bag.

She began her speech in a calm, deadpan voice. "There are people who say that when you go camping, you should take only pictures and leave only footprints," she said. "We wanted you all to have something that you could take away to help you remember this trip. Remember when I told you all that a camper's best friend is a bandanna?"

She held up a bandanna. "You can use it for a hat." She tied it on her head. "You can use it to wipe your nose," she said as she pulled it across her face. "It can be a napkin." The kids watched her with serious concentration. "You can use it to wash your armpits," she said, raising her arms. The kids laughed.

"Really, I'm serious."

"This," she raised a bandanna again, "could be a lifesaver."

In the city, it could be a flag of death. A bandanna was the rag that dangled from pockets, that segregated people by its color, that wiped the blood from hands from a gunshot wound.

"How do I look?" Lindy asked as she draped her black bandanna over her wind-frizzed hair.

John wrapped his yellow bandanna around his head and knotted it in a ponytail.

In our barrage of colored hats, scarves, headbands, and wrist bands, we looked like a group of forest bandits, whooping and hollering through the woods. We played Capture the Flag. We sponged our sweat, and we washed our armpits. A bandanna is a camper's best friend.

Lesson 5: Say Something Nice

"Yeah, you're ugly too," John said as he munched on his apple.

"John," I cut in, "Do you remember our agreement about negative comments? For every cut-down, you owe Veronica one compliment."

"Veronica? She knows she's ugly."

"That's two, Charlie."

Johnny wasn't being malicious; he just wasn't thinking.

"But there's nothing good to say about Veronica."

"That's three."

I laughed. Johnny wasn't getting out of this one.

"You mean you can't think of anything good to say about her?" Ms. Harper asked.

"No." The whole circle of kids started giggling.

"Four," they said in unison.

Rosemary spoke up. "Veronica always thinks of other people," she said.

"Yeah, that's one, I guess," said Johnny.

"Johnny," Ms. Harper said, "You have to give the compliment, not Rosemary.

"Veronica's smart, too," Humberto said.

"Yeah, and she's not afraid to run into the bushes even though there are thorns," said Denise.

"She was too stupid to look," said Johnny under his breath. He paused and then realized what he had said. "Miss, I didn't mean. . . !"

"Five. Boy, Johnny, I guess I am going to have to go into your homeroom and make you write out a list of compliments for Veronica."

"No, Miss! I'll say them, I just have to think of one. . . ."

We waited.

"Wellll, she . . . she . . . she lent me a pencil once."

"That's a start. Four."

"And she has a nice smile. . . ."

"Three."

"And she is smart. . . ."

"Hey! I already said that one!"

"Okay, she's intelligent. . . ."

"Two."

"Even though she didn't give me the answer to Number 10 on the math test yesterday. That really sucked."

"Three."

"Okay, okay, she keeps me from cheating."

"Two."

"And I'm glad she came on this camping trip," Johnny said as he wrapped his arm around her shoulder.

"One, zero. You did it!"

Final Lesson: Expressing Thanks

"Hey, everybody!" I yelled. Kids were running around rehashing an earlier game of Capture the Flag. "We need to do one more thing before we leave." We gathered in a circle, and Ms. Harper began handing out purple and blue note paper.

"We need to thank everyone who helped put this trip together."

"Like who?" Johnny asked.

"Carlos Trejo got us the van . . . ," I began to say.

"He also drove a new van up late last night so we could make it out here," Lindy said.

"Ben packed our lunches; Trinity helped to pay for the sleeping bags and tents," Ms. Harper said. "There are a lot of people to thank. . . ."

As the kids got their pens, they disappeared to find a quiet spot to think. . . .

I am writing to say a BIG, BIG, BIG, "Thank You." The field trip was real fun. Did you know that this was the first time I went camping without a restroom?

Thank you for coming with us. I had a great time. You really know your way around the woods. I was really glad I was on your team in Capture the Flag. I didn't think you could run that fast.

We hiked down trails and up what I would call mountains. We slept in sleeping bags which were in tents. I personally loved it.

Right now I'm looking at a beautiful mountain view thanks to you. I really appreciate all you've given to Earth Corps to help sponsor our trip.

This is my first time going camping. It was so cool. At night we sat and sang songs. We ate some funny food, but it was still good. I guess because I didn't wash my hands, or I must have been starving.
P.S. Don't litter.

A Frog Needs Only To Be Kissed

Alice, our team leader, launched into a new topic by saying, "Oh, by the way, Raymond Arias is being sent back to us from the Frog Pond." The teachers—reading, social studies, math, history—and I, the intern, looked at our English teacher.

"Raymond Arias?" The history teacher asked in disbelief. "What happened?"

"The Frog Pond said that with his poor attendance and attitude they couldn't do anything to reach him," Alice answered.

"Well, that makes sense—can't control a kid in the Frog Pond with 15 students in a class so put him back into regular classes with 35 plus kids. Makes perfect sense to me," my mentor teacher, Patsy, answered in a voice that was slowly raising its tempo and southern twang. Patsy, above all of us, was discouraged with Raymond.

Raymond was a temperamental firecracker; he sat, dead silent and still, and blew up at random instances. But he was not dangerous. At 4 foot 2 and 42 pounds, Raymond wasn't a physically menacing boy. I never had gotten the impression that he would strike out at someone. Even his verbal outbursts were defensive rather than offensive.

Each day was a new adventure in teaching Raymond. I say "teach"; actually, I mean "control." In rare instances, Raymond shone with the luster of an achieving child. Most times, though, he carried on his duties as the classroom time bomb.

In the beginning of the year, there were a lot of confrontations.

Patsy had the voice of a true southern woman. She would speak to both the President of the United States and the janitor in that same respectful, chipper voice. But in anger, her tone flared and she could bark orders that made even our principal hesitate.

"You ARE going to keep your head off your desk!" Patsy pulled Raymond's slumped shoulders from his desk and his head swayed on his neck. His eyes sleepily squinting at the light, Raymond put his hand to his face and gave a lazy yawn.

Patsy touched his shoulder and spoke softly into his ear, "Did you hear me? I said you are not going to sleep through my class." Raymond suddenly woke from his hazy nap and jumped to his feet, flinging Patsy's arms from his immediate space.

"Don't touch me, man! Don't ever touch me!"

"I don't want you sleeping in my class," Patsy repeated. "Do you want to fail seventh grade?"

Raymond's stance now righted itself. "I don't care, man, just leave me alone!"

Clank! . . .

Bang! . . .

He had punctuated his statement by throwing his chair to the floor, and then he skidded to the back of the room. His shoulders slumped, he began toying with the pencil sharpener.

"Raymond! . . ."

"Don't talk to me. I told you I don't care!" Raymond's face turned to the back wall, away from Patsy and the rest of the class.

"Raymond, please come back up here and sit down."

(Pause)

"Come sit down!"

(Pause)

No response.

By now the rest of the class was absorbed in the confrontation. Eyes focused on Patsy. We all wondered, what next? Patsy turned her attention to the 35 other students and said, "If you don't finish your assignment, do it for homework."

She went to her desk and pulled out a referral form. I began circling around the room answering student questions. Raymond remained at the pencil sharpener.

Two minutes passed, and . . .

Bink!

A paper clip flew across the room and struck the front table. It came from Raymond's direction, but before I could turn my head, I heard an "Ouch!"

Another paper clip had found a softer target. Raymond had leaped to the other side of the room and was banging on Angel's desk while talking. "Raymond, leave this room immediately!" Patsy's voice boomed. Raymond, for once, complied. He was gone for the day—out of the room and down the stairs. I looked out the window and saw him stride to the Conoco across the street.

Whatever confrontation we had with Raymond, whether it started out polite and quiet or in shouted commands, the script was always the same: Raymond would fly off the handle in some way and would eventually storm out of the room after repeatedly disrupting the class. He would spend a few days in the alternative center and then would reenter the classroom to begin the cycle again. The vice-principal quit responding to our referrals on Raymond so we began ignoring him if he slept in class. Better he not learn than the whole class be distracted from the lesson.

Raymond was labeled *at risk,* an all-encompassing term that described students who, for one reason or another, did not function well in a regular classroom. It included the withdrawn, the violent, the socially inept, the unmotivated, and, especially, the unpredictable students. We nominated him for a position opening in the Frog Pond, a specialized cluster of students and teachers in nontraditional, small classes. Frog Pond was named, so they said, because a frog needs only to be kissed once or twice to become a prince or princess.

Raymond went.

Raymond returned.

He was "hard to work with," Frog Pond teachers said.

Maybe Raymond was emotionally disturbed (ED). I tended to think so. Maybe as teachers we should have kept documentation on Raymond to get him tested. Then again, Raymond wasn't a special case. For example, Melissa was withdrawn; she didn't speak more than two words in a week. Juanita would turn in one assignment in 6 weeks, and when confronted, would shake her hair over her face and shut down. James would work only if I physically placed a pencil in his hand and sat beside him, hand on his shoulder, and encouraged him the entire time.

I could go on. There might have been 50 or so of my 160 students who should have been tested for an emotional disorder.

What child at age 13 is not emotionally disturbed? Adolescence isn't an easy period.

So which one should I have started documenting? I couldn't have done them all. The counselors wanted 6 weeks of behavioral documentation from three teachers, and then *maybe* the student would be chosen to be tested and placed on the waiting list, and by next year (after we passed the kid to the next grade) the school would get results back.

It doesn't really matter; a child labeled ED is still ED. The counselors have stacks of ED files on their desks. No one has time to deal with them. The lists only grow longer; nothing really changes.

Is there an answer? I wish I had time to spend with each of my students. They all deserve individual attention and encouragement, and some will work only with specially designed lessons. I have, on average, 35 students during a 40-minute class. That gives me only 1 minute and 17 seconds per student. I end up teaching a very utilitarian class—the greatest good for the greatest number of students.

So Raymond slept through seventh-grade science. Every once in a while, he woke up and decided to participate.

Raymond wasn't stupid. I taught a very traditional unit on study skills, and even though he didn't turn in any daily assignments, he (gasp!) got a 100% on the test. No, he didn't cheat; I checked his paper against the student he sat next to during the exam. The other kid failed. I'm not sure what it was that reached Raymond. Like I said, every once in a while, I saw a glimmer of intelligence.

At that point, it was all I could ask for.

Earthworms

"Well, are we ready for dissections?" I asked Patsy. It was March. We had been building the kids' lab skills for dissections all year. Seventh graders had to learn how to work in groups, stay in groups, be quiet enough to hear instructions, and take responsible care of lab equipment, themselves, and the desks.

"Well, we are going to find out today and tomorrow. You never know. The last intern I had got a probe stabbed into his thigh." Patsy raised an eyebrow as she took a breath and continued, "The weird thing is, the kid that did it was usually nice and calm, never threatening. I saw him. He just picked up that probe and jabbed for no apparent reason."

I held up a rusty probe labeled #5 and touched the point with my fingertip. "We had better be ready."

First period hadn't started yet, and we were organizing the lab equipment into their numbered sets. I laid the #5 probe down on the #5 plate. Tomorrow we would be adding scissors and scalpels to the supplies.

A swarm of students entered the classroom. Questions rained on me from all directions:

"Can we get into our groups?"

"Are we doing a lab today?"

"Do we sit in our groups?"

I waited for a break in the downpour and answered, "No, sit down in your regular seat until we take roll." Two seconds later, I was again pelted with questions:

"Where are the worms?"

"Where have you got them?"

"Can we see the worms?"

I puffed my cheeks full of air, turned to the questioners, and pointed at my mouth, "MM MM MM MMM MMMM!" Laughter. They were satisfied for the moment.

It took 8 minutes after the bell rang to take roll, get the kids into their lab groups, and get them calmed down enough so I could give instructions.

"Okay," I said. "Your Materials person will come up to the table. Get the equipment with your group's number on it, get a lab sheet, and take it back to your desk. Get two damp paper towels and place them on your plate. After all that is done, I will come around with your worms."

"Remember!" I said, "*Today* we are looking at the *outside* structures and the behavior of the earthworm. We'll look at the *inside* of the earthworm *tomorrow*."

"Are they alive?" Bernice called from the back.

"Yes, they are alive. Please do not torture them, and I would like to get them all back at the end of class, alive and well. Do you all understand?"

"Yes."

Although we had been studying worms for days, in their excitement, kids were forgetting my prep work.

I turned to get my box of worms and then back to the kids. "What is the probe used for? Stabbing, jabbing, or poking?"

"No, it is used for moving and touching," Johnny said.

"Come on Miss! Where's our worms?" The suspense was killing them.

I opened my box. "Remember, no 'EEEW's, especially from you girls."

Eyes followed my every movement as I picked out each worm from the box and draped it across each plate. As more worms made their debuts on group plates, the classroom grew quieter and quieter. I had never seen them this calm. I started circulating around the class.

Johnny was touching the worm with the point of the probe. "Which end is the head?" he asked.

"Well, which way is it moving?" I asked.

Johnny said, "But it's moving both ways, Miss!"

I moved to the next group. They were also using their probe to coax their worm into motion. I raised my voice to talk to the whole class, "You know, sooner or later you are all going to have to touch your worm."

I got a look of shock from some, smiles from others.

"You mean we can pick them up?" Sarah's hand was frozen, mid-air, ready at the signal to pick her worm up.

"You are going to have to when you get to Number 6 on your lab instructions."

"I ain't touching no worm," I heard Bernice's piercing voice say. Everyone was still absorbed in introductions.

"Don't forget," I said to the class, "to follow your lab instructions. By now you should be on Number 3."

Groups began shuffling papers and organizing their study. Question 1 asked whether the group's worm was male or female.

I crossed the room to a group who had begun scribbling answers on their lab sheet. "So, do you have a boy or a girl?" I asked.

Leslie looked up from probing. "A girl."

"Na uh," Robert said, pen in hand, "A boy."

"Well, which is it?" I asked. Then Robert remembered.

"It's both!" He turned to his group. "It's both!"

I moved on to the next group. They were already on Question 6, which asked them to feel the top and bottom of their worm, and describe what they felt. Christy had the worm on the back of her hand and was rubbing it with the tip of her finger. "The top is smooth and slimy," she said.

"What is the bottom like?" I asked.

She turned her worm over and rubbed. "It's rough!" she said.

"Those are the bristles, or setae, we talked about yesterday," I added.

Christy let the worm crawl up her arm as she scribbled notes on her lab sheet.

I went to the next group. "What is a sensory organ?" Carlos asked.

"You have sensory organs," I said. "How do you know that there is a worm in front of you?"

"My eyes."

"How do you know what I am saying to you?"

"My ears?"

"So how does your earthworm know what is around it? Does it have eyes?"

"Yes."

"It does? Where?"

Carlos looked at his worm. "It doesn't have eyes!"

"So how does it know what's around it? How does it find food?" I asked as I moved on to the next group.

Bernice's voice rang through the class again, "I want to kiii—ll it!"

I walked over to Bernice. Her eyes were a bit glazed as she stabbed at the Styrofoam plate with her probe. The earthworm, as if sensing impending danger, was stretching off the plate and crawling under an opened book.

"I want to see its insides," Bernice continued.

"Tomorrow, Bernice. You'll get to dissect tomorrow. Why don't you give the probe to Henry for a while?" I asked.

The probe dropped to the table. "Here Henry," she said.

Eva approached me. "Miss," she said, "What will happen if I put two worms together?"

"I don't know. What do you think, Eva?"

"Maybe they will rub together and mate!" she answered, sliding her hands back and forth.

"Well let's see!"

As with every lab period, the end of class came quickly.

"Okay y'all, let's get things wrapped up," I said. "Make sure you get all your questions answered."

A cluster of students had formed around Eva's experiment. "Eva," I said, "What happened to your mating worms?"

"Nothing happened, Miss," Eva answered in disappointment.

"Why wouldn't your worms mate in this situation?" I asked.

"Everybody's watching!" Christy answered.

"That's one good reason," I said. "Many animals won't mate while people are around. Think of some others while you clean up. The bell's about to ring."

I got my worm box and went around collecting specimens. Christy gave her worm one last pet. "Goodbye!" she said as it dropped into my collection.

The equipment table was almost refilled. "I need number 4, number 3, and number 11's plates," I said, "You have a minute and a half. When the bell rings, turn in your labs on the corner table." Kids were scrambling to get everything done.

The bell rang.

"Bye Miss!" Everyone called as they rushed out the door.

Silence passed over the classroom, but only for a moment.

A swarm of new students entered into the classroom.

Questions bombarded me from all directions.

"Can we get into our groups?"

"Are we doing a lab today?"

"Do we sit in our groups?"

Another class had begun.

The Tapestry

Begin with
Small, fragile threads.
Careful!
Do not stretch too far or
Some threads may . . .

. . . Break.
That happens sometimes.
Don't sweat it.
Usually you can
pick up the pieces
and retie them.
Sometimes too many
threads break
and you get discouraged.

But set it down
for a while,
Concentrate
on another part
of your tapestry,
You will get back to it.

The tapestry
is all connecting.
The tapestry
is everything,
it won't disappear.

If you want to make
an intricate design,
You need to spend

some time building
the threads
into strings,
or even ropes.
Wrap the ideas around,
gather
and
twist them together.

Sometimes it helps to
group similar colors.
Colors can complement
each other.
But don't worry

if your color scheme
doesn't work,
You never know
if colors clash
until
you get them together.

Well,
then there are
the Reds.
They tend
to bleed all over
the Pastels . . .

If you get tired
of a motif,
pick up
another strand,
focus
on another design.
This tapestry isn't a
uniform, one-colored,
one-designed piece.

This tapestry
is a busy patchwork
full of holes
weak spots,

stains.
But it is also
Unique
and beautiful in parts
The colors so vivid
and varied.

And it is a Tapestry.
One continuous art form
One continuous classroom.

TWO

Ms. Harper

*"One thing they never teach you about teaching is that
it's best not to teach."*

Güera

✳

I stuck my arms behind my back and held onto my fingers. Suddenly my hands made a dive for my front pockets against the stiff fabric of my khaki skirt. A full gymnasium of seventh graders eyed me over. What should I do with my hands? The thought became painfully conscious. I pulled my hands out of my pockets and tried to force them to my side, but they jumped up to my hips. No, I thought, too authoritarian. Or was it authoritative? I couldn't remember the difference, just that Dr. Waldron had said that it was important to establish clear rules and consequences from the first day of school.

"Patricia Aguilera!" The voice of Geoffrey, my mentor teacher, boomed over the echoing chatter in the gym. Here we go, I said to myself. It was the first day of school, the fabled and magical 7 hours when everything must come from nothing. *Ex nihilo.* The only problem was that *I* was the nothing, for it was not just the first day of school. It was my first day as teacher.

I remembered my own first day of seventh grade—the cheerful but serious letters from teachers that I had to get my mom to sign, the long lists of school supplies that I should carefully buy at Randol Mill Pharmacy on the way home. I remembered trying to decide whether to buy a three-ring binder or a clipboard. I remembered knowing that the rules and punishments listed on the letter home didn't really apply to me and my friends. They were there for the bad students who didn't care.

"Adam Aguirre, Melissa Arriaga," Geoffrey continued calling out names from the computer printout. He struck a pose in the middle of the semicircle of seventh-grade teachers. I stood beside him and slightly behind. Patricia walked forward reluctantly, an old binder at her side. She had long black hair with bangs arching forward a few inches above her forehead. Then came Adam, a skinny boy with jeans drawn up around his hips. He looked 4 or 5 years younger than Patricia. No Melissa yet.

"Arriaga," Geoffrey tried to say again, but his mouth didn't work fast enough. It came out "Araga." He smiled a wide smile and leaned his weight on one hip. "Ah . . . Ree . . . Ah . . . Ga," he shot out one syllable at a time. The names even scare me, I thought. And so many of them.

One by one, our new homeroom class bunched together in the middle of the semicircle, each student trying not to be at the front of the bunch where the unclaimed seventh graders would stare at them. I groaned inside my throat, suddenly confronted by the snapshot my mother had taken of me on my first day of junior high. The image made me cringe. I had a new perm and new peach-colored jeans. Only last year, when I was digging through my scrapbook, did I notice that in the picture my fly was wide open. Seventh grade was definitely a spectator sport. Each new name drew moans and sighs from the other seventh graders.

"Heradio Flores, Maribel Flores, Ralph Flores, Rene Guajardo." The names sounded completely foreign to me. Shackelford Junior High, my alma mater, was filled with names like Karen Meador and Brad Davidson and Kate Austin and (the best to make fun of when I was twelve) Jimmy Pickulenski. Not one of my friends was anything but white, Anglo, and Protestant; not one had divorced parents, not one was poor, and not one was even Catholic. My best friend, Karen Li, was Chinese, but she seemed so white that I forgot that she was technically a "minority."

"Claudia Ortiz. Rudolfo Pecina. Rene Rodriguez," Geoffrey continued, visibly enjoying his role in the spotlight. Geoffrey could command even a gym of rowdy 12-year-olds without straining his voice. He sounded like a black preacher, which, in fact, he was. Mrs. Banasau from the Eagle team had rolled all of her r's, but I didn't think I would be brave enough to try to fake it. To make matters worse, Mr. Reyes had gone before Geoffrey, and had purred each name with a Mexican accent.

"Reuben Rodriguez, Edna Ruiz, Cindy Sifuentes, Adam Urena." Geoffrey had finished the roll call. The last two kids strode up to the bunch. Our new homeroom, I thought, and I tried to keep the mask over my face: Don't let the fear show; don't let the shock show; don't let me look like an out-of-place white girl.

Shared Inquiry

Dr. Holtz wants to observe me teach fifth period today. Good. He'll see it as it really is, and he won't wonder why I ask all the wrong questions during our pedagogic class.

I draw my class into a small circle of about 10 desks in the middle of the room. Dr. Holtz folds himself into a desk next to Richard and leans over to look at Richard's book. Please don't let Richard have any obscene gestures sketched in his book, I think to myself and walk toward the circle. Today will be our second class discussion on "Harrison Bergeron," which Great Books calls "shared inquiry."

My face and neck feel hot as I give instructions. "Get out a sheet of paper and write down this question." It is a simple request. I never try to be too creative with fifth period, because they can't settle down. I just try to be clear and stay in control.

"Get out a sheet of paper and get ready to write down this question: Do you think Harrison represents a danger to society or the savior of society?" I say the question more than ask it; after all, I'd already asked it during second, third, and fourth periods. I break the question down into bits and try to repeat the bits slowly.

"What?!" Raymond demands. "Wait! What did you say?"

"Raymond, you know I'm going to repeat it," I answer. "James, why aren't you writing?"

"Can I have a pass to go to the restroom?" Maria whines in a loud whisper.

"No."

"Why not?" she whines again.

Back to the question, I tell myself. "Do you think—" I pause. "Harrison represents—" I stop. "R . . . E . . . P . . . R . . . E . . . S . . . E . . . N . . . T . . . S . . . Do you think Harrison represents—R . . . E . . . P

... R ... E ... S ... E ... N ... T ... S ... Do you think Harrison represents ... ?"

"Miss, why can't I go to the restroom? I've got to go!" Maria pleads, almost yelling. I feel Holtz's eyes on me, watching what I will do.

"Maria, write down the question. James, write down the question. Veronica, write down the question."

This is a shared inquiry? I ask myself. I don't even know what we are sharing or inquiring into. I do know that I will not let fifth period run over me again.

Self-Portrait From a
Rough Wooden Desk in a Circle

Spinning in circles
I catch. I dart. My eyes poke
and hover and smile.

Across No-Man's-Land
past Miss's bent-over waist,
whisperings scurry.

Each desk spins by in
orbit, pulled together by
I still don't know what.

Only that I reshape
the circle with the clanging bell
and spin it again.

Or maybe I'm It

flailing my arms
in a game of Keep Away?
Here! Throw me the ball!

Over here! I can't
help you with your writing when
I have to babysit.

I can't babysit
when I have to help you with
your writing. I'm dizzy.

Here! Let me play, too.
I lunge. The circle blurs and
I miss and I land

squarely in a rough
wooden desk in the circle
and tuck myself away.

Didn't I?

If I don't look up, maybe I won't cry. If I don't cry, maybe they'll see that I'm trying to handle this professionally. If they think I'm handling it professionally, maybe I *can* handle it professionally.

If I handle it professionally, maybe it won't hurt so much.

I shouldn't have said it. I shouldn't have raised up my arms and laughed and smiled. Then, I could say that they had misunderstood me and that they were wrong. Just wrong. But the scene plays in my mind again and again. I see myself raise my hands in the air and laugh the indicting word, "Hallelujah!" I bet my face looked so stupid to them, so open and happy.

The scene begins to replay again:

Chairs crowded around the long table, looking as though the wooden armrests could pinch any fingers that rested there. Briefcases and notebooks cluttered the table, and another class meeting of EDUC 695 had begun. The Twain interns crowded the back corner, eating Cheetos Puffs and laughing about our own failures.

The worst possible time to schedule a class for teachers had to be 4:30 in the afternoon. We came coated with chalk and ink and failure and wanted only to become clean again. So we drew to each other and whispered our confessions and tried piously to discuss higher things.

"Does anyone have anything they'd like to share this week?" Dr. Holtz began.

I began. "Well, one of my students withdrew today." I looked around the table. Karen sucked on her water bottle. Jeff and Jeanette poked each other and tried to stifle a laugh. Dr. Martinez sat at the end of the table, hands folded and eyebrows raised.

"Emilio Garcia."

I said it slowly and loudly, halfway thinking that just the name itself would explain everything. "Hallelujah!" I said, stretching my arms and fingers and laughing.

Cheers rose from my corner of the room. Someone patted my shoulder. Kathleen gave me a knowing smile. She had him in science class.

"He was a terror. He came from a drug rehab hospital," I explained, shaking my head. More nods and cheers. I didn't even wonder if everyone understood.

I had forgotten it when, 30 minutes later, an intern leaned forward and looked down the table at all of us.

"I don't want to be mean or rude when I say this, but there seems to be a growing number of us who are starting to be . . . real negative? We're talking about being *glad* a student withdrew. What happened to the beliefs we all seemed to have this past summer?"

Silence. I clicked my ballpoint pen closed.

I stared down at the tweedy fabric of the chair, the way the chocolate threads looped over the tan ones. I pushed the ends of my fingers into the wooden armrest of my chair. My fingernails whitened. I let go. Purple and pink flooded back in.

Finally, Kathleen spoke up. "How can you say we don't care about the kids? You don't even know what it's like to feel physically threatened."

I remembered Emilio's big body and the way his eyes flashed when he taunted me.

She continued. "How would you feel if a kid turned in a paper, and all it said was, 'I want to kill a teacher' written over and over?" She stared down at the table.

The scene continued to replay in my mind. I kept my fingers pressed into the armrest. I tried to listen to the words as if I were overhearing someone else's argument, but my stomach was knotted and my knees pressed tightly against each other.

I didn't want to let them hear me defend myself. Too much suspicion. Too much pain. I didn't care about the kids? The accusation had been sweetly made, to help us reflect on our teaching, I suppose. But no one understood, and I felt my chest burn with bitterness.

Jennifer shoved her chair back and hurried out, head tucked down and crying. The rationalizations poured out.

"We're just frustrated."

"We deal with so much during the day."

"Yeah, we bring it here and we gripe too much."

"She didn't really mean it."

But didn't I? Shame floods my face. I could have hidden it better, I guess. But can't I care about my kids and still be glad that Emilio is gone?

I'm Out

I'm out a camera,
nineteen dollars,
a box of black ball points,
a bag of Brach's pick-a-mix,
three red and blue spirals,

and a whole night's sleep
while I watched Whoopi
and read and coached with a blue felt tip
and heard the first news of David Koresh
and wondered if I was in a strange dream.

And wondered why, even in a dream, I would stay up all
night and read and coach with a blue felt tip.

They steal from me.

Robert Castillo even stole a dream from me.
(He was laid out on his back, unconscious,
and I gave him mouth-to-mouth.)

Why, even in a strange dream, would I surrender
myself and my stuff and my chance for an earful of
Yes, ma'ams, quiet whispers, and busy pencils?

But I steal from them too.

It's my secret.

I didn't know it myself
until I fell out of a desk during second period,
until I taught Jaime that cemetery is not spelled "semen-tary,"
and saw "Miss Harper #1" in pink bubble letters on the board.

I borrow and they borrow, and we forget to pay back.

Hearing Their Voices, Part 1

October 4

Fifth period is now my least favorite class. My stomach gets tense during lunch and doesn't let up until fifth period is over.

Even as I fight my way up the stairs to my classroom, the kids shove and yell. My head hurts, my throat aches, and I am not in the mood for any deviations from my lesson plan. My students, riled up by lunchtime gossip and basketball, always are.

In this battle, I see only the bad. I ignore the quiet majority— Audrey, Mary, Nancy, Albert, Jorge, Hector—that probably wants to stand up and scream at everybody. I forget that I have to keep Richard, Ricardo, Raymond, Maria, and Veronica on my side, or they will fall to the enemy camp in seconds.

The bell rings, and I walk through the doorway. I begin making sure all the students have their pencils and spirals. They don't. I begin making sure everyone's quiet and listening. Hardly.

Am I being paranoid?

October 28

It has gone too far. Fifth period is not listening to me. They're not getting anything done. They're making me feel stupid. This will stop, I tell myself.

I feel ready for the deciding battle. I hand out a Xeroxed list of rules and consequences. I read the rule out loud: Respect yourself, respect each other, respect the teacher. Simple.

I start to discuss the rewards.

"Let's decide what our class can work toward, what reward we'd like to earn," I say, moving over to the chalkboard to tally their ideas.

"Let's listen to music or go outside!" Raymond calls out.

"Pizza party every Friday!" Davonne yells.

"Yeah!"

"No, that sucks!"

"All right, get quiet." I stand and wait. "Get quiet." I stand and watch. "Don't lose your reward before we've even decided what it'll be."

"Pizza every Friday!"

"No more writing!"

"Hey, fifth period," I called. "We also need to decide exactly how you will earn this reward. For example, I was thinking that you would have to go for two weeks without getting any time after the bell."

"That's impossible! We'll never get that." Raymond actually laughs at the idea.

More noise. More arguing.

"Hey, you guys! At least pay attention long enough to decide what the reward's going to be," I yell into the maelstrom. "Don't lose your reward on the very first day!"

October 29

Raymond was right. Fifth period had to stay 3 minutes after the bell today. They already lost their reward. The problem is, they know and I know that I'm beginning to get desperate.

December 5

I sit in one of the desks in the circle. It's hard to give directions from a small, graffitied, wooden desk, but it seems important to sit there.

"Spend the next 10 minutes writing in your spiral notebook about anything you want," I tell fifth period. I glance around the room one last time. Jorge rocks his desk back one last time. Raymond and Ricardo hunch over with laughter at some secret joke. James lies with his head down. "I'm going to be writing too, so get busy."

I open the folded, fat, pink spiral notebook that I had started on the first day of school and I write. I don't even look up.

I'm wondering what it will take for fifth period to become the kind of class that it can be, that it really wants to be. I picture a class that is made up of 24 individual writers—

young adults who have something to say from inside. I want them to be able to describe what they're going through— their pain, fears, excitement, frustrations. I don't want to feel like their dictator, but like another writer. I don't want to feel like their dictator.

Words of Wisdom From the Front Seat

He tossed the big manila envelope on top of the copier.

"Have a good holiday, Laura," he said, as casually as he had tossed my grades at me. Then he strolled out of the teacher's workroom and down the main hall. I pulled out my evaluation and flipped to the back page. Neat red print slanted across the bottom. "Course grade: B."

The copier had stopped. I set down the paper. I ducked my head out the door and watched Dr. Holtz stroll away.

"What?" I whispered to myself. I let out a short, whispered laugh. I heard sounds from the auditorium: "The First Noel, the angels did say, was to certain poor shepherds in fields as they lay." Christmas music. I blew all the air out of my lungs.

Mrs. Purnell walked in to use the copier, but I was still leaning forward on it, staring at the neat red lettering.

"Well, have you made it through the Friday before Christmas?" she asked in her southern sing-song.

I laughed, but my eyes stung. "I got a B." My eyebrows pinched together.

"What? For what?"

"My grade for the internship," I said flatly.

"Why?"

"I don't know. I thought I'd get an 'A.' I've done my very best."

"I think you all should get A's. What did Kathleen get?" She switched the subject.

"I don't know. I haven't talked to anyone else," I replied, already feeling the bitterness creep into my voice.

"So you're a teacher?" the cab driver asked me from the front seat. Two weeks had passed; the blessed Christmas break was quickly running out. It had been 2 weeks since I had to discipline a class or think of a lesson or drive into the teacher's parking lot at Twain. Two weeks with no dreams of students, no papers to grade. In fact, it had been 2 weeks since I had really felt like a teacher.

I looked at the way the taxi driver's hair caught on the knit collar of his ski jacket. I tried not to catch his eyes in the rearview mirror.

I should never tell anyone that I teach, I told myself. Here come the speeches.

He tossed his comments at me over his outstretched arm that bent backward to rest on the seat. I was only trying to get from the hotel to Denver's airport. I already felt tense just talking about teaching, for I had only 2 days left of Christmas break.

"Well, I've got a friend who teaches sixth graders here in Denver. He tells me all about it. From what he tells me, it sounds horrible. You know what he says about those kids?" he asked, already laughing at his own joke.

"What?" I asked impatiently. Words of wisdom from the front seat, I thought to myself. Just what I need.

"Those kids' hormones are on GO, and their brains are on NO!"

"That's about right," I said, almost to myself.

"You know what else he said?" We turned into the airport, and I tried to tune the man out, ready to end the conversation and pay the fare. "He says you can't teach unless you love the kids. That's the only reason you'll go back each day. You can't do it for any other reason."

Something in my heart jumped. My face felt hot despite the cold air. I grabbed my bags out of the driver's hand and awkwardly stuffed some bills into his hand. "Thanks," I said, and began my trip back to San Antonio.

Hearing Their Voices, Part 2

✳

January 25, 1993

One thing they never teach you about teaching is that it's best not to teach. Fifth period taught me that. Today, I'm enrolling in the School of Fifth Period, and today I'm finally learning.

"We're going to be starting something new these 6 weeks," I began, looking around the circle. Lord have mercy, I thought, but I adopted a tone of confidence and excitement. "We will be transforming this classroom into a writing workshop." What was I trying to do here? They're not writers . . . they're not even humans.

Raymond stared down at *Where's Waldo*. Michael was engrossed in an elaborate pencil drum solo. Edwina powdered her nose and under her eyes.

"Listen to me, you guys," I said, trying not to lose it before we even started. "We're starting something completely different, something you never get the chance to do in your other classes."

A few heads turned to face me. Veronica slugged Edwina, and Edwina slid her compact into her back pocket.

"What, Miss . . . chew gum?"

"Huh? We can chew gum in here?" Michael asked, drum solo over.

"No, you guys. It's bigger than gum. I'm talking about the entire classroom, the way we do things in here, who makes the decisions."

Jorge put his desk to rest on the floor. Raymond glanced up from his fruitless searching for Waldo. Even I got excited.

"I'm new at this, too," I told them. I truly had no idea what I was doing, so I got busy handing out papers while I tried to explain. "We'll all be writing in here. In fact, that's what we'll do all period long. You'll come in and tell me what you want to do that day. Did you hear that? *You'll tell me* what *you* want to write about."

Wow, I thought, that does sound good. A community of writers. We'll read and write and discuss and share.

Across the room, I see Mary look over and smile at Gladys. I could tell she was already imagining what they could write and talk about. Well, at least 2 out of 24 are hooked. Two down, 22 to go.

January 26

Today, it's all clicking.

"Aw, man, I told you I don't understand that part. Why does that guy in your story . . . Chris . . . say that it's too early to rob the store?" David pleads. "It doesn't make sense."

Raymond tips his desk forward and smiles. "It's too early because they want to wait until the store's almost closed."

"Well, then, you've got to say that. Right, Miss?"

I lean against the door frame and try not to laugh. I listen to the conversations around me. Yes, they're loud and they're talking and they're laughing. But they're learning. My students are involved in their writing, I say to myself and shake my head.

I'm finally hearing their voices.

Fifth-Period Voices

"My Baby"
by Jesus Morales

I was scared to be in there with my girlfriend. It's not that I didn't want to; it was because I was nervous to see what was going to happen. I couldn't believe I was going to be a father.

I was so nervous that I couldn't talk to the nurses and the doctor. I was always holding her hand while I was in there. She was going through a lot of pain. She was holding my hand tight and screaming loud. She cried for a long time. From what I saw, I wouldn't like to have a baby, especially with all those needles they gave her.

The room was full of people and weird machines. One machine had lights to see when the baby was coming out, another with the I.V. on it. I saw a table with knives, needles and scissors. Everybody was busy doing something in there. After she was born, I was asked to leave and wait outside.

It felt good holding my baby in my arms, and I know I have a lot of responsibility. Her name is Blanca Marie Morales. She's white, with blond hair and blue eyes. She looks like her mother a little, but more like me.

from "My Dizzy Day"
by Beatrice Aguilar

My face felt hot and was probably as red as a tomato. I could feel sweat running down my forehead and neck. I felt dirty and gross. All of those people were staring at us.

The gym was filled with echoes of cheers, shouts, and screams. The cheerleaders shouted the best they could. The eyes fell on me because I was about to serve the ball.

I felt like I was going to miss the ball. All of a sudden, I started to feel dizzy. I kept on seeing two balls. I didn't know which one to hit. Then, everyone started to be quiet. I felt my knees shaking. The sweat ran down my forehead and around my neck. All of a sudden, it stopped or paused. My arm was paralyzed. I couldn't move my arm to hit one of the balls, and my knees wouldn't stop shaking. There was no more sweat around my neck or forehead anymore. It seemed like I was imagining things.

All of a sudden, I swung at one of the balls. . . .

from "The Summer of Joy With Love"
by Diana Lopez

Claudia Chavez, Anthony Vasquez, Gloria Mendoza, Mark Rios. I mean, the names kept on going. I was hoping to myself, Please don't let my name be announced. I don't want to go to summer school.

Sure enough, though, my name had been called. . . .

On that first day of summer school, I met a lot of friends who were boy crazy, and I was in love with a boy named Manuel. He was in the eighth grade. When I first saw him, right away, it was love at first sight. At least for me it was. That same day I had met a friend who sat right in front of me. Her name was Laura.

"I bet I'm going to get Manuel's phone number," I told Laura.

"No, you're not," Laura said.

She was right. He got mine instead.

from "A Gun at School"
by Adam Sanchez

"Oh man, what's this for? I don't want this thing. Where's Humberto?"

"He got busted."

"How?"

"He was unloading the gun. Then—BANG! It went off," he said.

Then all of a sudden he pulled out the gun. It was a nice, dark, black, shiny, wanna-be-polished gun. All of a sudden, I snapped.

"Hey, give it here before someone sees it, or put it away." I just hoped he would put it away. Instead, he gave it to me, so I put it away scared that someone would have seen it.

Next thing I knew, one period went by. It was sixth period. Then the principal, Mr. Johnson, walked in the class. He whispered to the teacher, and right then and there I knew I was in trouble. I started to gather my belongings.

"Adam, come with me. Get your books and let's go," Mr. Johnson said. When we got outside, he asked me, "Do you have something you're not supposed to have?"

"Yes. Yes I do," I said.

"Can you put it in my pocket?" "Yes, sir." I did it.

"Okay, let's go."

from "Nothin' Could Be Worse Than This"
by Ray Zamora

I woke up. I got dressed for school. I put my shoes on. I ate my breakfast, and I looked at the clock. It was 7:55. I freaked out, so I hurried to catch the bus.

I missed it! When I hit the school grounds, I noticed I hadn't combed my hair. I even noticed I didn't have socks on.

I was late to class, so I got lunch detention.

I finished my history exam. My mind was going nuts.

If the weather could match my mood today, I thought to myself, it would be terrible. Cars would fly out of driveways. Trash cans would flip over. Windows would shatter. Dogs would drown. People would be on boats.

I don't think anything would ever match my mood on a day like this.

from "Don't Trust No One"
by Raymond Smidt

"All right, I'll go in. You keep the motor running. I'll tell the clerk, 'This is a stick up. Give me all your money.' If he doesn't, I'll pull the trigger and blow him away," said Chris.

"All right. I'm in," said Mike. "Are you?"

"I . . . I . . . I don't know," I said. I paused for a moment and said, "Okay." We headed out to the store. Chris waited for a few customers to leave. Then he said, "It's show time." He stuck the gun in his pants. He went inside the store.

"What do you think about helping Chris with the stick-up?" I asked Mike.

"It's cool," said Mike. The next thing I knew, I had started the engine. I heard a loud gunshot. I thought Chris had wasted the clerk, but it was the other way around. The clerk had wasted Chris.

from "A Return to Pimplicity"
by Monica Vasquez

"Class, today we're watching a movie about pimples and how to deal with them," said our teacher. I was in second period, Mrs. Delgado's class, Home Economics.

She started the cassette. The movie began.

"Hey, Cheryl! What's up? Where are you going on Saturday?" said Beth.

"Oh, I'm going to the school picnic," said Beth. "And you?"

"Oh, I'm not going anywhere!"

"But why?" asked Beth.

"Well, just look at me. I can't go anywhere with these pimples."

I thought to myself, Well, what else can Beth do? I kept watching the movie. Beth was saying to Cheryl, "Come over to my house. I have Clearasil, and you can put it on. You have to clean your face every day."

"Oh, I'll do that as long as they come off," said Beth. When she said that, I thought, Yeah, I'll do that too.

The movie ended. Everyone was stunned as if a bee had just bitten them. The teacher turned on the lights.

"Okay, class. So what did you learn?" Mrs. Desmond asked.

"I learned always to keep your face clean," I shouted.

"Well, yes," she said. "The bell's about to ring, so I'm going to pass them out."

"What?" people in our class asked, not understanding what she was talking about.

"The Clearasil stick," she said.

"What?!?!" everyone yelled. We started giggling. The bell rang.

"Wait," the teacher shouted. "Tomorrow, we're playing Bingo, and, if you win, you get a pack of Clearasil!"

from "He Didn't Care"
by Nancy Trevino

My dad decided to leave us. He started packing his bags.

"Don't go," my mom said. I went into the room my dad was in, and I started to cry.

"Don't go. Please don't go," I told my dad. My mom came into the room.

"You see, even your daughter doesn't want you to go," she said. I left the room and started to cry. Then I heard my mom and dad arguing again. My mom said, "Why do you want to leave?"

"Someone said that you were going out with and talking to another man," my dad said.

"I've never gone out to see other men," she said. When I heard that fight, I thought it was my mom's fault. Then my mom said, "You're the only man I've ever gone out with."

"I'm leaving," my dad said, and he finished packing his stuff and went into the living room. Then he went towards the door.

My mom started crying. I started crying.

"Don't leave, Dad. Don't leave, Dad," I said. He left anyway. When he walked out the door, I felt like he didn't care anymore, like he wanted us out of his life.

One Brown Leaf

by Trudy Lucio

One brown leaf
falling from a tree
in the middle of the night,
and one child
looking from a window
and no one else
would even know.

Humbertoandrene

I sat sorting through the rubbish left on my desk by a chaotic fifth period: absentee slips, behavior contracts, suspension papers needing my initials, leftover handouts, late homework.

"Miss Harper," Humberto began, Rene close behind him. Humberto Gonzales and Rene Roldan were a pair, and, by sixth period, pairs meant trouble.

"Yes, guys?" I answered, not looking up. I heard a bubble pop. "Please spit out the gum, Cathy," I said over the growing noise in the room. I heard a sticky plunk in the trash can by my desk.

"You know the valentines we're making to send from a god to a goddess or a goddess to a god or whatever? Ya know?" Rene started.

Humberto took over. "Wul', we were thinking about doing, wul' we want to do it the three of us . . . as a team," Humberto interrupted himself as he spoke. He pointed at George across the room. In the middle of my line of sight, Joey and Joe were stabbing pencils in the air conditioner vent.

"Joey and Joe!" I called through the din. Knowing they'd been caught, they went to their desks. "Humberto and Rene, what do you need? The bell's about to ring," I said, looking at the clock and then at Rene.

Rene had such long eyelashes that they put a smudgy shadow on his face. If I were in seventh grade, I thought, I'd probably have a crush on one of these guys. I always did like the boys that talked and talked and talked, and wrote weird poems and wore the same t-shirt day after day.

I started to worry. Did that mean that I *liked* Humberto and Rene, that I had a crush on two 12-year-olds? I decided to be up-front.

"You know who you guys remind me of?" I asked, leaning forward and smiling. I knew I was about to freak them out.

"Who?" "Who?"

"Henry Stone, the guy I had a crush on in seventh grade," I announced and raised my eyebrows to wait for their responses.

"Blech!! Miss!!" Humberto dodged to the other side of the room and threw his books into the bottom of his desk. "Yuk!!" Rene laughed and followed him. After a short conference, they came back again. They had decided to ignore me.

"Wul', anyways Miss, you know how Zeus can send a valentine to Hera, or Psyche can send one to Cupid, or . . . " Humberto paused out of breath to look at the other choices on the chalkboard behind me. I could tell he was trying to avoid the dangerous implications of the Henry Stone comparison. " . . . Or Hades can send one to Prospero, or Poseidon to Demeter, and the other way around?"

I got out of breath just listening to them.

"Yes. . . . " I waited.

Humberto looked back at Rene, so Rene took over. "We want to have Zeus send one to Psyche instead of to Hera, like he's seducing another woman; and then we could pretend like Hera finds out, and so she'll send one to Cupid to tell him that Zeus and Psyche are having an affair, and so. . . ." Rene paused. Even he had become tangled in his thoughts, and he squinted up at the ceiling trying to untangle them.

"So then Cupid sends a really mean valentine to Zeus," Humberto said, making the save.

"Can we do it that way?"

The two of them stood proudly across my desk with their arms at their sides. Finally at rest.

I paused, enjoying their silence as they waited for my decision. Of course I would let them. Their idea sounded great. This was the kind of idea I dreamed my kids would think of. But I would have to make them think that I was *really* bending the rules, that they were getting special privileges. That way, they'd work even harder.

The bell rang. Adriana and Javier dived into their desks from the doorway. I acted like I hadn't seen them, although their desks slammed into the wall. I looked back at Humberto and Rene, an adolescent Push-Me-Pull-You. "Okay, I *guess* you guys, as a team, can work on making these three valentines. But I need to see some incredible rough drafts by the end of the period."

"Yesssssssss!" Humberto and Rene yelled in the flush of victory.

I laughed and came out from behind my desk to start class. It was Valentine's Day at Twain, and I had a crush on two 12-year-olds.

A Prayer

Why don't they listen to me?
God, forgive me for not quietly listening for Your voice.

Why can't they think in new ways?
God, forgive me for being scared of change and risk.

Why can't they be individuals?
God, forgive me for following everything except You.

Why won't they see that I want what's best for them?
God, forgive me for not trusting that You hold me in
Your hand.

Why can't they enjoy each other?
God, forgive me for my gossip, jealousy, and discord.

Why don't they learn from their mistakes?
God, forgive me for being defensive about my
weaknesses.

A student is not above his teacher, nor a servant above his
master. It is enough for the student to be like his teacher, and
the servant like his master.
—Matthew 10: 24-25

When I Think They're Listening to Me . . .

(from a note taken up during seventh period)

I suffer from despair
not knowing if you'll be there.

My tears come down in fear wondering
if you're mine.

I shake in terror knowing you belong
to another.

Give me pleasure by becoming my
treasure.

The Good Times

Why was it so hard for me to write a good story about my kids? Why can I think of all the hard times, and so few of the good times?

We noticed it at our last group meeting. All of Corinne's stories were the happy ones, and all of mine were so sad.

"My stories all end with 'Okay, I'm a loser and I don't know what to do about it. Any questions?'" I realized, sitting cross-legged on the conference table in the education classroom.

"I think it shows something about our personalities," Corinne suggested.

"I don't know," I came back, eager to dodge the label of cynic. And I wasn't a cynic. I bragged about my kids with the best of them. But why, then, was it so hard to write about the good times?

My mentor Geoffrey and I always laughed while we walked from lunch back up to our classroom.

"Let's go touch some lives," he would say, and we would laugh with each other. "I'll grow, and they'll grow, and we'll change each other. They'll touch our lives. We'll touch theirs. We'll learn and discover new things. . . . " We would shove our way through the crowds of lipsticked girls flirting with sweaty boys, through the line circling the water fountain, through the groups of kids at lockers plowing through paper wads and notes.

The lofty platitudes of teaching seemed crazy in a zoo full of seventh graders. "Yeah, *I'll* touch some lives," I always responded with fatigue.

But sometimes I did.

Cecie pounded her cymbal. Jorge flashed the overhead projector that created our lightning bolts. Sailors wearing trash bag raincoats ran across the stage screaming, and then crashed into the wings where I stood watching nervously.

"Miss, there are so many people out there!" Christie whispered. She almost knocked over the cymbal during Prospero's opening monologue, but regained her balance.

"Did we look okay?" Michael asked seriously. He was rewrapping shredded bags from the dry cleaner and strips of blue burlap around his head, and his eyes were wide open. Michael was an air spirit when he wasn't busy being a sailor.

"You guys looked great!" I shook my head. I couldn't believe how everything had come together. We were performing Shakespeare! Kids who hadn't passed their classes were performing *The Tempest*.

"Miss, is this picture okay?" Jaime whined. He shoved his book right into my face. I pulled it far enough away from my eyes so I could focus on it.

A stick-figure man was pulling himself out of a coffin, having just been struck by a crayoned lightning bolt. Jaime smiled at me.

"That's the man who kills all the people," he said, beaming.

"There's just one *problema*," I mentioned, not knowing how to handle this one. "See how you spelled 'cemetery'?" I asked, trying not to laugh. Jaime looked down at his book where a sign read "SEMEN-TARY."

"Jaime, go look the first part of the word up and see if you think you might have spelled it wrong," I suggested, about to die laughing.

A few minutes later, Jaime, evidently not having read the dictionary entry himself first, walked up proudly to me, pointed to the entry, and began reading.

"A sticky white substance . . . "

"Jaime!" I cut him off. "Do you see your mistake?" He turned bright red and ran to his desk eager to make revisions.

"Which way do I turn?"

"Left."

"Right."

"No, it's left."

"Rene, shut up. Miss, it's right."

"Guys, listen. I'm not taking you on a tour of San Antonio. Which way is it to your house?" I sighed. I knew the game Rene was playing. He had a huge crush on Jennifer, who was crowded in the back seat next to him, and he wanted the ride to take as long as possible.

"Miss, really, it's right," Ralph said seriously.

"Okay," I said, turning right onto North New Braunfels. Suddenly, I was surrounded by army trucks. I knew Ralph and Rene didn't live near Fort Sam Houston, but this was getting interesting. I glanced in the rearview mirror to see what was happening in the back seat.

Jennifer and Michelle laughed in the back.

"Really, Miss, this is the quickest way." Rene tried to sound convincing, but his eyes were glued to Jennifer.

"Drop 'em off here, Miss," Jennifer offered. She didn't find Rene as attractive as he found her.

"I'm about to," I said. The traffic light turned red. We didn't make it through the next green light.

"Look, Rene, Ralph, it's 4:36 now. When it's 4:40, I'm dropping you off wherever we are, so you'd better be getting us close."

Four minutes later, less two male passengers, Jennifer turned to me more exasperated than I was. "You should have dropped them off earlier, Miss."

"Here she is," Sandy said, beaming. She held her baby, Blanca, bundled in her arms. She brought her, I thought to myself; I can't believe it. During my last week at Twain, I had asked Sandy to bring her baby to school so I could tell the whole family goodbye.

Blanca was already 4 months old, but she looked like a preemie. A pink knit cap covered her head, and a thin cotton blanket held the rest of her body tightly together. I stood close and stroked the tiny hairs that escaped out of her hat.

"Do you know that your mommy and daddy are going to be famous writers some day?" I asked Blanca. "Yes, they are. Did you know that you're already the star of one of your daddy's stories?"

Sandy asked me if I wanted to hold her. I couldn't wait.

"Here you go, Miss," Sandy said, placing Blanca in my arms.

No story neatly ends. Especially the happy ones. They have no solution or resolution. There is no clear end result.

That frustrates me. I want so badly for my joy to be neatly tied up so that I can look at it admiringly, so that I won't lose it if kids head downhill. I want so badly to *see* my successes—I don't know, give me certificates or badges or jelly beans. Then I can stack them up, count them, and rate myself as a teacher.

That's the worst thing and the best thing about teaching: Things I really dream about as a teacher are the messiest and hardest things. Things like relationships, loose ends, pain, memories, conversations, and knowing laughter.

As crazy as it sounds, even to me, I now know that I teach so I can be involved in my students' lives, in their real life stories. The catch is that my students become involved in mine too.

They are my characters, they spin the plot, they cause the conflict. (Okay, I give them a little help here.) I was supposed to have been their writing teacher, but they taught me to write. I was supposed to have taught them about growing up and changing and loving, but they've taught me.

All that's missing is that neat resolution I urged my own students to shoot for. But as long as we're involved in each others' lives, there can be no resolving the stories, just listening to them.

THREE

Mr. Huntley

"To be a teacher you must be able to step outside yourself and look at the situation . . ."

Hemispheres Apart

Dedicated to Sylvia Lovelace

At 7:00 p.m., on the eve of my first day of teaching, I stepped back into the doorway of room 107 and looked in at my creation. I was alone at that point; Benita and Sylvia had given up on the project. They were satisfied with the piles of confusion and the slight disarray of the whole picture. To them, it hadn't looked all that bad.

Not me. This was my first day of teaching, ever! I wanted it looking perfect. For 2 more hours, I placed this here and stuffed that in there. I pulled desks forward. I pushed them back. I made temporary stacks look permanent. Someone has since told me that even God never proclaimed the world was perfect after his 7 days of creation. At that time, I didn't know just who I was competing with.

I stood there, in the doorway, and thought that it was good. The room was crowded with desks. There were 30, in six neat rows of 5, to accommodate nearly everyone we expected to have. The rest would sit at a long line of tables against the side wall. Our lists had some classes of 32 or 33, and though we did not know it then, we would very soon be teaching classes of over 40. There were stacks of brand-new books sitting on three odd shelves and a metal display rack. There was one small teacher's desk for the three of us who would be sharing the room for the year. And there was a wonderful set of cubbyholes on the wall behind the desk, already overflowing with odds and ends, in no order, mostly things waiting to be found and recognized as important.

But the real killer lurked in the corner. There was a benign looking partition concealing it, with pretty flowers all over it. However, at certain angles of approach, you could glimpse what lay behind it. It was a living, lurking thing, with cardboard teeth and dusty breath, laminated eyes, a bulk of boxes, books, and room decorations. It was the Beast. My nemesis. My worst nightmare.

I had created it out of necessity. My counterpart in the classroom, Sylvia, owned much of what became the Beast. At first, most of it was stacked in different parts of the room. Manageable nuisances, they were, and for Sylvia, another surface to put things on. I should have trusted her; she was, after all, the master teacher. I was the newcomer. But in haste and anxiety I stacked the Beast to the ceiling in that corner. I gave it the size and power to destroy me.

As I surveyed the room that evening, I saw it come to life. You'll regret leaving it here tonight, I thought. It will grow. It will eat you up one day. I pretended not to hear myself. On my way out the door, I carefully, quietly slipped up to it and scooted the partition a bit closer to it. I did not look back.

I don't think Sylvia ever really knew the monster I'd created. She used it as a storage shelf, a resource center. I couldn't believe that it let her tear things from its body so joyfully, resources for various holidays, units, and whatnot. Whenever I got near, it spoke to me. It said things like, "I am the outcast of your ordered universe. Have you ever faced the evil of entropy? Smell my musty breath! Witness my mass! You shall not rule for long . . . Ha ha ha ha ha!!!"

I suppose the Beast defined the difference between Sylvia and me. She was a right-brainer; I was a left. I had an unending desire for order in my classroom, and she, well, she just didn't worry about things like that. I couldn't understand how she could work in a room where piles of stuff grew like organic material. I couldn't fathom how she got things accomplished!

As the first month progressed, I coded the books and arranged them neatly on the shelves. I displayed their glossy covers as if the room was a B. Dalton store. We noticed that the kids were dying to get their hands on them, and we finally gave in. With 40 kids in the room, crammed into the regimented rows, we set out on an adventure using our independent reading program.

Unfortunately, there was no room to get comfortable. The room got incredibly hot with all those volcanic adolescent bodies sitting there. For most of those first few weeks we stood as three engineers in that room, trying to hold up a disciplinary dam around the seething bodies. Every day after school, I spent increasing amounts of time straightening desks and putting some semblance of order back into the novels on the bookshelves. The beginnings of left-brain fatigue seemed to be evident as I gave up on the alphabetical arrangement in the first 2 weeks.

After a couple more weeks, I was beginning to give up on everything. The discipline problems continued. The orderly environment I thought I had conceived was fraught with complications. For example, the back rows of the classroom were inaccessible regions from which paper and pencil pieces were hurled at vulnerable victims, and there were zones where, apparently, no teacher's voice could be heard. Fed up one day with the arrangement, I got to thinking and moved a desk.

Four hours later, that October evening, the room was unrecognizable. I always have a tendency for grandeur when I make changes. This time, I had reoriented the room toward a side wall. I had created an island of tables in the back, and a bookshelf that doubled as a teacher's podium in the front. The teacher's desk was gone, donated to Ms. McCready next door. The desks were in a U-shape, providing more access to each student. And I had been able to remove six of them. Now there were places to sprawl and read.

The books, however, still remained in chaos. Novels turned up behind shelves, on the sidewalks outside, and in the trash can. And still, at least once a week, I dutifully arranged them until I was satisfied. But something was happening. It was taking less and less for me to be satisfied. Was my cerebral dominance swinging toward the right?

It seemed as if on the grander scale of order, I still needed control. I was in that capacity a perfect match for Sylvia, because she did not mind my tinkerings with the room at all. "Just let me know where you put my things," she said to me. On the more immediate level of day-to-day maintenance—rearranging desks, books, shelves; keeping classwork—I was growing to tolerate the mayhem.

Actually, there was hope for me. I just might make it through the year, I thought. Only one more thing remained: the Beast.

The Beast had grown dustier and crustier, and had settled a bit. By November, it had become an established part of the room. No one but me noticed it anymore. I think it would have been there for the rest of the year, for all eternity perhaps, if one day Sylvia hadn't started talking about it again.

School was over, and Sylvia and I sat at the back tables, talking. She rose to find her holiday season decorations.

"Boy, this stack of boxes will probably be here until May!" she said with a chuckle, pushing through the middle of the Beast. "Too bad we can't put them somewhere. . . ."

I jumped at the chance. "Well, we can put some on top of the cabinets, and just go through them to see if there's anything to get rid of," I began. I looked at the Beast. It glared back at me. "What do you think?"

Sylvia was hesitant. Most of the stuff was hers. "Well, I think we could look through it tomorrow. . . ."

I made sure she remembered her comment. The next day, at 3:15, I approached her. "Well, shall we take a look back here at the Beast . . . er, the boxes?"

She moved over beside me. There was a pause. Was I going to have to make the first move? The Beast glared defensively at me. I stepped forward and grabbed a box. "Let's see what's in this one," I said.

Forty minutes later, I had done it. My heart pounded in victorious joy. The Beast was dead. Its parts sat in different piles. One was on top of the cabinet. Other bits were stacked behind bookshelves. A third pile was set to be loaded into the trunk of Sylvia's car. A small, baby Beast cowered behind the file cabinet, where its big brother had sat. I glared at it. It trembled.

The terror was over. Our room was now a place of satisfaction for two people hemispheres apart. There were no problems when I decided to rearrange the room a third time, to remove more desks and set up the Chapter 1 area. There was no more fuss over books scattered like fallen leaves across the shelves, or the right-brain "Pile-O-Dex" filing system.

Sometimes it takes a heavy sigh for me to be able to walk away from a "well-used" room, but I can do it now. As Sylvia and other right-brainers have told me, I've loosened up. Look at my room and you'll be certain of it.

But you'll never get me to admit it.

A Leap of Faith

In the fall of my intern year, I spent 2 days at a camp in the Texas Hill Country with students from Twain's alternative program, known as the Frog Pond. The trip was part of the YMCA Hy-Lyfe program at Twain, and sought to provide the at-risk students with trust- and esteem-building experiences.

I was counselor that weekend, not teacher. Corinne McKamey was my partner. We spent 2 days chasing eight students around Camp Flaming Arrow, in Hunt, Texas. On the first day, upon our noon arrival to the camp, we put the students in their groups. Corinne and I led ours to a wall beside the gym.

"All right, everyone, for the next day and a half, we are going to be a team," Corinne began. "We'll have to work together, and that means we need to cooperate. And we have to learn to trust each other. My name's Corinne."

"And my name is Jeff. Let's all introduce ourselves." I urged on the girl closest to me, sitting on the low rock wall.

"Jessie."

"Angela."

"Joanna."

"Eduardo."

"Ray."

"Leon."

"Juan."

Pause.

"And what's your name?" Corinne asked the slouching form at the end of the line.

"Daniel."

Daniel was much taller and bigger than the rest. He was a 16-year-old eighth grader. He was in a gang. The year before, his girlfriend had given birth to a baby who had died during delivery. He was angry at the world. He wanted everyone, including Corinne and me, to stay out of his way.

Later that afternoon, as we all observed ants busily moving to and from their subterranean fortress, a foot suddenly stomped down on the hole.

"Kill them, ha ha!" Daniel said, as he flattened the insects with his size-12 shoes.

"Daniel, that's inappropriate," I scolded. "Please stop it or you will have to sit down with me."

But as Daniel continued to dance on top of the poor creatures, there was really nothing the rest of us could do. He was shouting profanities at small red insects. He grunted with conviction after every stomp. His glare was serious and intentional.

His behavior seemed to stem from a burning inside, an anger that was larger than I could possibly imagine. He threw rocks at the wild turkeys and screamed at the deer. He played basketball in the late afternoon until he was completely exhausted.

On the second day, on our way to horseback riding, he decided to take off into the woods.

"Wooooo!" he shouted as he half ran, half tumbled down the steep slope thick with brush. He collapsed to a stop at the bottom, rose, and continued on his tear.

"Daniel!" we called. I couldn't see him anymore. Swearing under my breath, I went after him.

I stepped through the brush to the edge of the slope. I saw a white shirt dodging through the trees 50 yards away. "C'mon, Danny! You know you can't do this. They'll take you home right now!"

He stopped. He turned and ran to the right. I stepped out of the brush and cut around the wooded area to head him off.

He emerged from the trees a few yards from where I was waiting. "Danny, we need to get with the group," I begged. As he stood and looked around him, ignoring me, ignoring my interests, the YMCA director drove up in her car.

"How's he doing?" she asked me quietly. I shook my head.

"Come on, Daniel, get in the car. I'll take you back to the gym," Martha called to him. He continued looking around, shifting his weight from foot to foot. It didn't seem as if he had heard, but he suddenly moved to the rear door of the car. He opened it and got in.

Martha smiled at me, and as the car drove off I saw her head turned back to him, mouth moving.

I thought that was the last we'd see of the angry young man. We all thoroughly enjoyed horseback riding without him. Most of us had forgotten the frustrations of Daniel's presence as we approached the Challenge Course, our final activity.

I heard Martha's voice behind me first. "I think Daniel would like to join you all for the final activity, if you don't mind," she said.

Daniel stood beside her, looking at his feet.

"That's great!" I offered. Most of us were tired. The rest nodded their heads.

I became flustered as we attempted the teamwork-building exercises of the Challenge Course. Hearts weren't in it. We barely succeeded on the "elevator," an exercise in which we had to fit everyone onto a small wooden platform at once. We failed on the "burning building," trying to get everyone across the wooden beams to the other "rooftop." By the time the "trust fall" came around, I was ready to quit.

In the trust fall, each member of the group was to take a turn falling backward off of a 4-foot-high platform into the outstretched arms of the rest of the group.

Me trust these small kids I had gotten to know yesterday? My body was saying, "No way!" My heart was racing. As others took their turn, I played an important role, as one of the stronger, heavier members, in catching them. "Don't panic—just relax and trust us. We'll catch you," I offered, not really believing what I was saying. Would I have to do this? I wondered.

Then it was my turn. "I need all of you to do your part, okay?" I looked into all of their eyes. My eyes stopped at Daniel, who stood several inches taller and broader than the rest. "I trust you!" My heart was pounding. I turned around, looking upward at the finger branches fracturing the white sky. The branches became a blur and I closed my eyes, falling rigidly back into the air. . . .

I felt a web of arms cradling me, and opened my eyes. Daniel was smiling down at me. "Yeah!!!" I cried, in absolute euphoria. They had saved me. The trust worked. I knew who had to go next.

"Daniel, if they can catch me, they can catch you. I won't let you fall."

He paused for a moment, looking down at his feet. He nodded his head, moving over to the platform.

"Okay! Everyone! We've had enough practice. This one's going to be easy. Yeah!!" I again yelled. Adrenaline was surging through me.

He looked back over his shoulder at us, and without a second thought, dropped straight back into our arms. "Wooo!" he let out his favorite war cry. I pulled him up with one arm and high-fived him with the other. He was grinning. I felt very proud of him.

Corinne and I lingered back a bit from the troop as we walked over to the council ring, where we would be giving each of the kids an award for some special quality within them. At lunch we had decided upon the awards for our students, but I felt that one change was definitely necessary.

"Corinne, after the trust fall, we have to give Daniel the Trustworthiness Award."

"But what about Joanna?"

"Well, we can easily find another for her. She was wonderful. She'll never know, and I'm sure that Daniel deserves it."

We made a quick change and continued to the council ring.

When it was our group's time to announce its awards, Corinne and I took turns announcing them. I stepped forward and called Daniel's name.

"We weren't really sure which award would be best for Daniel until the final activity. When we did the trust fall at the Challenge Course, Daniel made me a believer in the whole group. I knew I trusted all of them then. And when Daniel took his turn, and did not even seem to be afraid, I knew he deserved the trustworthiness award. Congratulations, Daniel."

The applause around us was distant from my ears. I smiled at Daniel, and he smiled at my feet. He walked back to his seat, clutching the small colored bead that was his prize.

I needed no other reward than witnessing his participation earlier in the trust fall activity. However, it moved me moments after the conclusion of the ceremony, when he came up to me.

"Thanks, Jeff," he said, clutching my hand in a firm shake. His grin was neverending. With a look back over his shoulder at me, he headed up to the bus.

Daniel made me a believer in the human spirit. Beneath the anger and the fear, no matter how intense, Daniel carries with him a sense of the need we all have for faith in one another. His soft "Hey, Jeff" as we passed in the halls for weeks afterward was a reminder of the special connection we had made.

I found out in early spring that Daniel was moved out of Twain to a special school because of violent behavior. Some day he may be put behind bars because he "can't be trusted to live in our society." I think we just need the right time and place to give him a chance.

T.G.I.M. (Thank God It's Monday)

I thought I vowed I'd never see
What today ran over me. . . .

Pillow and pencil fights
Violated computer rights
Abhorrent sights,
Like:
A student jumping out of the window
(I didn't see who it was, though);
Outrage that cause brought detention effect
After running and screaming left concentration wrecked;
"Read!" can never work as a command
Especially when classrooms get way out of hand . . .
Out of sorts. . . .
From:
Breached trust;
Teenage lust;
Now I must . . .

> *go on.*

The last group came
And they were—the same.
Did I treat them fairly?
As they screamed and fussed? Barely.
I took one aside
And could not let it slide. . . .
I called his mother.

Then I sat with this boy, trying to be a man
To escape the classroom's peace-and-quiet ban
He's devoted to friends, and scoffs at school—

The fool!
But gets threats for colors on shirts, shoes, and pants
He rants—
Why do you care?

Why do I care?

I was born to—hey, life is unfair.
I may get ulcers and gray hair,
But on Tuesday morning. . . .
I'll be there.

Learning to Laugh

Dedicated to Benita Longoria

Ms. Russel and I were skipping down the hall, arm in arm. Near the office, we passed three of my students, who watched in amazement.

"Sir—you're weird!" Hector said. Oscar looked away in humiliation. Sammy's jaw was dangling near the floor.

In response to such encouragement, Ms. Russel and I began to sing: "Weeee're . . . Off to see the Wizard! The wonderful Wizard of Oz!" We stopped our mayhem when we reached the north staircase and headed up. I took a glimpse back at our audience. The three boys were stumbling over each other, laughing.

"Sir, why do you like to embarrass yourself?" my students often ask me. They are completely terrified by the idea. After all, they are adolescents, at the peak of self-consciousness. Well-adjusted, mature adult that I am, my answer to them is that being laughed at is a refreshing reminder that I am only human.

My wise mentor Benita once told me that this attitude is essential for the teaching profession. "To be a teacher," she once said to me, "you must be able to step outside of yourself and look at the situation. And to be a great teacher, you must be able to laugh at it, too."

For that advice, I will be forever grateful to Benita. It is the reason I am still the same, well-adjusted, mature teacher today. Whenever I encounter a struggle that leaves me frustrated or angry, I now search for the perspective that trivializes my hurt pride.

Case in point. One afternoon in seventh period, lesson plans crashing and burning around me, Carlos took my pen from me and would not give it back. I stumbled around the table after him, my anger growing with every step. Keeping just out of my reach, Carlos yelled, "BOY, SIR—YOU'RE OUTTA SHAPE!"

Everyone was watching the sideshow, so finally I stopped and said, "Carlos, give me the pen, now. You are disrupting this class for everybody!"

Carlos looked at me with his squinty eyes and baby face. His grin broadened, and then he began taking an informal survey.

"Am I bothering you?"

"No."

"Am I bothering you?"

"No."

"See," he said, throwing up his arms after he had asked everyone. "I'm not bothering anyone!"

I was surrounded by laughter. Students watched my reddened face expectantly, to see how I might further make a fool of myself. But I surrendered to the mob, joining them in a good laugh at my expense, my self-respect, for the most part, still intact.

Some teachers may sooner draw the line on what is acceptable behavior in a classroom for either student or teacher. But good humor has a power to it that I am just beginning to understand. I have even put it to use in my curriculum. On the day I started my poetry unit, for example, the fifth-period kids were particularly rowdy—just how I wanted them.

"Can anyone remember what onomatopoeia means?" I asked.

"Huh?"

"A what?"

"Who cares!"

I cut in as the talking began again. "Onomatopoeia are words borrowed from sound," I said, but there were so many examples of the term going on that no one could hear me. No one was listening anyway.

I watched the talking and joking continue as I grabbed the largest dictionary in the room. I held it out in front of me. I let it go.

WHUMP! Following the noise there was a shocked silence.

"What did that sound like?" I asked, enjoying the surprised, confused looks.

"Boom?"

"Bam!"

"WHAM!"

"CRASH!"

As the students' enthusiasm again began to fill the room, I grabbed the next sound generator from my pocket, a party favor I had brought with me. I blew into the noisemaker. The curled-up ribbon shot out into the din.

BZZZZOOO!

This time, there were expectant, thoughtful looks in the audience.

"What was that sound?"

"Honk!"

"Hoot!"

"TOOT!!"

As a flock of deranged ducks took over the room, I honked with them. I laughed. And I was disappointed that I had to settle them down and continue. I wanted to make more fun noises.

Laughter is my secret weapon in the crusade to break down barriers between teacher and student. Every day, I try to show my students that humor can be a part of the tasks that need to be accomplished, and that a good sense of humor develops confidence in one's self-identity. Without laughter, I know I could not survive, and would not be who I am—a well-adjusted, mature, 22-year-old kid.

Acquainted With the Night

The holiday magic arrived a week early.

At 10:00 p.m., in the final hour of my longest day at Twain, I was surrounded by enchantment. Strange music. Unusual signs. On the surface of it all, it was just a late evening in an old middle school building. A date between me and a temperamental copy machine. But as I walked down the upstairs hallway, munching on my Tom's Deluxe Cheese and Crackers Dinner for One, I knew there was something more to this cosmic alignment of me, the middle school, and a newspaper deadline. I had been chosen for something. And very soon, I would discover what it was. . . .

It all started with the curse. Early in the first semester, I had a strange compulsion to stay hours after school, really doing nothing more than puttering around, straightening up. Maybe some spell had been cast upon me. Maybe it was a potion put in my lunch one day. There I would sit, watching the school empty, listening to voices subside and hearing the mysterious noises begin.

I called it "The Transformation." The noises had something to do with returning the school to some semblance of order and cleanliness in the darkness of the night: squeaky wheels rolling down the hall behind soft sneakered footsteps, a rustle of plastic, soft sweeping noises traveling past my door, then gone. Sitting there, after school, I felt like I was chosen to be a witness . . . to . . . I don't know what.

After school on the Thursday before holiday break, I realized that my day had come. It didn't happen that morning, when I heard that Gwen Wilson, the faculty advisor for the paper, was absent. Nor did it happen when student after student involved with the paper came up to me, informing me that they could not stay after to finish the issue. And at 3:05, when it was just me and Stephanie putting together the holiday issue of the *Twain Times*, I was still ignorant of the revelation soon to come.

We worked efficiently, lost in the enormous task before us. Copy lay strewn in loose piles across the table. Scissors whispered around the words and pictures being assembled. The gluestick flew between us like an enchanted object. We talked a little, and I repeatedly expressed my gratitude to Stephanie for staying to work.

It wasn't until 4:15 that I realized my time had come. Outside the two doors to my classroom, I began to hear the familiar sounds of the Transformation. Surely something was going to cause Stephanie to disappear soon, for I knew with self-righteous certainty that whatever was going to happen would happen only to me.

"Sir, I've got to go. . . . My dad'll be here soon," Stephanie said in the next instant, as if on cue. Fate was in motion.

"Well, I appreciate your efforts. Maybe I'll put only our names on the staff list!" I joked. "See you tomorrow."

"Bye." She slipped out the door. I returned to the cutting and pasting, taking breaks occasionally to do some last-minute typing. Night crept in through the windows. Any lingering voices inside or outside the building had vanished. I flipped on the lights. I worked and waited.

There was movement outside my door at around 6:30. Banging and heavy footfalls. Some monsters had come to test my fortitude, to try to scare me away. A sudden buzzing and screeching erupted from just beyond the thin wooden barrier. Black smoke began to curl up from the space underneath.

I stopped my work. What was THIS?! I was not terrified, but rather annoyed. The acrid smoke began to make it difficult to see in there. I tried to continue, cutting and gagging, gagging and gluing. An ash-like dust began to settle on the paper. I stood there, one minute, two minutes, listening to the banshee in the hall. I was in a trance, probably induced by the toxic cloud pumped into the room. I was certain the monsters would soon be coming in to take me away in my stupor, to sacrifice me to the evil copy machine. I shuddered.

Suddenly, there was silence. I snapped out of my daze and decided to brave the hallway to see just what the heck was going on. I stepped quietly into the hallway through the other classroom door, half expecting elves to be pushing things here and there, tightening this, sweeping that. But there was no one. Just me, the music, and the dust formations.

A carnival-like sound drifted from somewhere above, probably on the second floor. I couldn't make out the source; it had bounced off so many walls that its substance was unrecognizable. Looking down, I noticed the formations. Small galaxies of dust, gum wrappings, paper wads, and pencil shards had coalesced in eerie swirls down the length of the hallways. They could not have been natural occurrences. Someone, or something, had made them. I carefully walked around them and headed to the end of the hall, searching for a glimpse of the demons who had been fighting outside the door to my room.

I should have known I wouldn't get to see them. A black plastic curtain, seemingly impassible, had been erected in my path. It was silent beyond. No need to call out and invite an attack, I decided. I turned the other way and made my way back to the room. Time to wrap up this immense project.

It took another 3 hours. I worked hard and long, carefully getting each page aligned right. It's just my nature to be thorough and neat. I wouldn't want anyone to do a half-assed job for me. And the end product was well worth it. A beauty. The best issue yet, I thought. Knowing now that there was nothing to fear out in the enchanted evening air of the school, I strode fearlessly out of the room toward . . . the evil copy machine.

Without surprise I saw that the black curtain, and whatever it had hidden, were gone. All that was left was a carefully carved line through the floor tiles, marking out where a handicapped ramp was soon to go. Ignoring the beckoning carnival from upstairs, I marched down the main hall, noticing that some dust swirls had merged into denser swirls, and others had disappeared completely. Still no sign of the mysterious beings who had done this work. Something had to happen soon. I couldn't take much more mystery.

I walked into the copier room. There it was, probably some administrator or teacher turned into a Xerox machine by an irked colleague. Its mouth was the small readout screen that seemed to smile when informing the user, "Paper jam. Check all areas and press C to continue."

"Nice copier," I said, patting it on the feeder tray. I entered my code and set it up for the job: 100 copies, one-sided originals to two-sided, from the auto-feeder tray. I took a deep breath and pushed start.

Twenty minutes later, I had only 30 copies. After two copy miscounts and five paper jams, it was finally running. I decided to risk leaving it to its business so that I could get dinner from the vending machine and call my roommate to tell him I was being held hostage in a middle school by forces beyond my control.

So there I was, at 10:00 p.m., in the upstairs hallway, crackers in hand and crumbs on my lips. Standing there at the top of the central staircase, poised to head downstairs. But once again, I became mesmerized by the enchanting music drifting down the hall. I gazed down the fluorescent-lit, shiny corridor, unable to determine the source of the song. My feet began to move forward. If the keepers of this mystery weren't going to let me in on what was going on, then I was going to find out for myself!

As I approached the end of the hall, the sounds grew more intense and focused. No longer a jumble of voices, the song became clear. The words were . . . Spanish! And beside the water fountain outside Ms. Harper's door, there was a small radio. It was Tejano music. Not fairies' incantations. Just the radio.

Okay, I thought, but that doesn't explain the dust formations or the weird noises. Or why I was here at 10:00 at night, for gosh sakes!! There had to be a big secret out there for me to unravel!

A little frustrated and very tired, I headed back down to the copier. I prayed that the machine had finished the first 100 copies. As I headed down the stairs, I heard the cheerful voices just below. Five men in brown shirts and pants surrounded me when I reached the bottom of the stairwell. Their conversation had stopped.

I felt like I'd interrupted some secret meeting. They all looked at me, probably thinking, What's the fool doing here at this ridiculous hour?

I mumbled something like "Got to grab the copier when it's available," and rushed past them to the copy room, fingers crossed. The room was silent when I got there. Sure enough, the screen read, "Copy miscount." But it did make 88 of the 100 copies. Not too bad. Well, if I can get 70 more out of it tonight, I'll be happy, I thought. I patted the machine encouragingly. Just get me 150, and I'll call it a night.

As I stood over the busy machine, I wondered if the custodians were all waiting out there because they wanted to close the building. Great, I'm probably holding them up, I thought. I put on my jean jacket and gathered my things. I stepped out into the hall and paced a circle to give them the impression that I was almost finished.

They were still standing in a circle at the stairwell, chatting. I realized I had not seen them actually doing any of the cleanup work.

They glanced at me. Well, I thought, what do they have to prove to me? I don't belong here this late. I had been toiling away during these unrecorded hours under special circumstances, getting the newspaper ready for tomorrow. Like magic, it would appear clean and fresh in a stack on Ms. Wilson's desk. She'd never know how much work went into it.

"Looks good," I could already hear her say. She would hand a stack to two or three students, who would sell them at lunch. Grabbing hands would take them for the low, low price of 50 cents, and eyes would pore over the pages.

"Good, the paper's out," people would think, like they do about the coffee always ready to drink in the morning, or the lunch served without fail at midday, or the mess that has vanished every morning from their classroom floor.

That was it, I realized. That's why I was here! I had been initiated into the invisible armies of the night, the saviors of order. I had become one of the secret organizers, doing work which, to everyone else, seemed like magic. . . .

I looked up, and a custodian was smiling my way. "You should be asleep now!" he said with a laugh.

I smiled and nodded my head. "Very soon—I hope."

It was 10:30. The front door clicked shut behind me. It was very cold outside, probably in the upper 30s. But not too cold for some of the heartier crickets, who sang to me out of the darkness. San Pedro Avenue was quiet at the moment. Behind me, there were no custodians in sight. They had vanished somewhere. They didn't see me leave. In fact, I realized that they never really saw what I was doing, either. And I wasn't surprised.

In the moonlight, as I headed hastily for my car, I saw something sparkle on it. Something was on my car. Oh, great. Some nighttime mischief. What a way to end my longest day ever.

Small things glistened on my car's hood, roof, and side window edge. And with disbelief I picked one up. It was candy! I looked up at the school, now in near darkness. I felt like someone in a "Do You Believe in Santa Claus?" movie. What was this supposed to mean? The weirdness of it all, or just my sheer exhaustion, allowed me to suspend my disbelief that night. I crunched on a sourball and chewed a Tootsie Roll as I drove home.

Tony the Camaro

Tony's middle name was Camaro, probably inspired by the classic car that was silk-screened across the front of his favorite black t-shirt. He arrived the second week of school, and on his first day was turning on his charm for the giggling girls of fifth period. Students that day took turns introducing each other to the class. The boy introducing Tony read from his notes that Tony loved eating pizza, playing basketball, and thought the girl sitting to the right of him was cute. From that moment onward, he had a captive audience in room 107.

Tony was a big kid. He was on his second go-round in sixth grade, but was easily as big as me. In his first few days, I did not think he would be anything more than a charming class clown. But my perspective soon changed as I watched Tony begin to take control of the classroom, over other students, and even myself.

Fifth period was my toughest class, but Tony never really needed the help of anyone else to conspire against me. He had a commanding presence, and when he shot out a comment, everyone waited anxiously to see what would happen next.

"Sir!" he would exclaim, slicing into my lesson and concentration. "Sir!"

"Tony, please," I would say, trying not to look like I was begging.

"Sir—Annie's crying!"

"Tony—"

"Look! She's got bugs in her hair!"

The class roared, Annie cried, and I could only wait until the incident petered out. Tony slouched back in his desk, or chair, or against the doorway where he had been made to stand, gazing over the spectacle he had invoked. He giggled with pride.

If anything, Tony was damn good at what he did. I hope I am someday as good a teacher as he was a class clown.

I can admire him in a twisted way now, but at the time he was more than I could handle. His persistent, businesslike attitude about class disruption wore me, and other teachers, down. I stopped giving him detention because he would just laugh heartily at the threat. He ran out of the building at 3:05; he ran out of detention if you turned your back. It meant nothing to him.

I didn't like the hatred toward Tony that was growing inside me. My ego and I waited for him to make his mistake, and finally, one day, it happened.

As I was teaching, he stood up suddenly and hurled a piece of chalk at Annie. The piece hit her squarely on the forehead, bouncing to the floor amid laughter from the class. As Annie sobbed, I dropped what I was doing, wrote up the incident with conviction, and sent a protesting Tony to the principal's office.

Next period, the assistant principal came to my door, beckoning me outside. I stepped out into the hallway expecting to hear the administrator say, "You'll have to take care of it." Instead, I saw Tony leaning against the wall, face red and mottled from crying.

"Tell him, sir, it wasn't my fault! You know other people were doing it! Tell him!" Tony yelled at me in a cracked voice, tears streaming down his cheeks.

I felt a sense of power over him for perhaps the first time in my life. It was exhilarating. I had stricken fear in this boy's heart. Confidently, I reaffirmed my position.

"Tony, I saw you stand up and throw a piece of chalk that hit Annie on the forehead. Other chalk may have been thrown, but I saw you."

"All right. That's all I wanted to know," the assistant principal said with a gleam in his eye. I could tell he shared my satisfaction. He looked at Tony and said, "He's upset because he knows his daddy's coming to get him."

As the semester passed, I felt myself becoming a fear-inspiring taskmaster. My most successful technique with Tony was shouting him into his seat, where he would then sulk quietly. Once in a while, my conscience would find its way back through the testosterone, to face me with a question it was becoming difficult to answer: Whatever happened to your warmer philosophies of classroom management? I searched guiltily for a response. Classes were quieter, weren't they? I was teaching more and shouting less. Shouting louder, but less. I struggled to balance the equation.

My thaw began just before the holiday break. I was sitting in the library at 7:15 a.m., listening to the choral group sing in a circle around the P.T.A. faculty breakfast. My mind was slowly coming awake, but I sat bolt upright as my eyes fell upon Tony, singing enthusiastically with the rest.

I couldn't take my eyes off the sight. A smile found my lips. At that moment, however, his eyes met mine and he stopped. I nodded at him and turned away. Suddenly feeling like I'd invaded his privacy, I got up and left the library.

So there's something that Tony likes about school, I thought. I imagined that he would never want me to know. After all, I was something he hated about school. If I mentioned his singing to him, he would never tell me about it. If I were to encourage him, he'd probably quit. The thought made my heart sink.

As I indulged in self-pity over what I'd become, I decided that I would renew my understanding of this young man named Tony Camaro. I would start by becoming a secret fan of his favorite school activity.

A few days later, Benita caught Tony idly singing a Christmas carol while sitting in class. When she complimented him on his voice, he clammed up. After a pause, he told her, "I'm going to sing in the Christmas pageant."

Although I was anxious to see many of my students perform in the pageant, I held the most excitement for Tony. On the day of the show, I watched Tony moving through the halls with lighter steps than usual. He asked special permission to sit beside the girl he was courting that week, and acted like a gentleman the entire time. I did not make any effort to encourage him or draw attention to his good behavior. I watched Tony and felt good that there was meaning in his life at Twain.

Benita met me at the auditorium door that evening. We sat down together and talked about Tony as we waited for his big moment.

When the chorus filed in, we looked for his head to be attached to one of the white shirts with bow ties in the line. My heart sank. He wasn't there. Although the performances of several of my other students provided me with a wonderful, moving evening, the reason I probably won't forget it is that Tony never made it.

I found out the next day, when he did not come to school, that he was suspended for fighting and, as a result, was not permitted to perform. I wanted to believe that he was as hurt as I was that he did not get to show a side of himself that may have renewed our faith in him. I imagined that he was kicking himself because he alone was to blame. Now, I would not see him until after the break. He'll probably forget the whole thing and come back, same as usual, I thought.

When he did return in January, however, he was not quite the same as usual. He was more lighthearted. He seemed less like an adolescent on a mission to drive his teachers crazy, and more like someone excitedly passing the time away. In a few days I found out why.

When I tried to persuade him to do his work one afternoon by telling him he was failing, he simply said, "That's okay. I'm moving." His dad had gotten a job in Floresville, he explained, and they were just waiting to find time to make the move.

My first thought was, He's lying. A few seconds later, recalling his change of behavior, I decided that, at the very least, Tony believed what he was telling me. Someone had made a promise to him. Tony was leaving!

I felt only pleasure in the thought. Not because I hated him. I was beyond that. I felt now that the entire situation of Tony's presence at Twain had passed the point of resolution. He had been written off by most of his teachers. He probably had no idea how to get on the right track, and since he was not wanted anyway, what was the point? He seemed anxious and ready to leave. I wondered if he realized that his escape from Twain was an opportunity.

I knew I would be setting myself up for disappointment if I were suddenly to encourage him or show any positive interest in him. As it was, I had actually begun to laugh more often at his antics. I saw that this adolescent had a personality that had incredible potential. I decided that I would lay myself on the line for him just before he left, and perhaps he'd take some new attitude away with him.

At the midway point of the fourth 6 weeks, Tony announced that it would be his last week. I prepared my progress reports so that he would receive his before he departed. When I gave it to him the day before he was to withdraw, he paused in seriousness for a moment while reading it, but never revealed to me his reaction.

During first period the next morning, there he was, standing in front of me, the familiar three-color carbon form clutched in his hand.

"I need my grades, sir."

As I had done so many times before, I dropped everything I was doing to accommodate him. As usual, all eyes were on Tony anyhow.

I wrote a 68 in the box by my signature. "But you can bring that up easy, right?" I asked him.

"Thanks," he muttered, grabbing his form, and was off to his next former teacher.

I saw Tony one more time before he left. On my way to the copier during seventh period, I passed Tony and his mother, talking outside the administrative office. I smiled at them, but didn't know what to say.

"Mr. Huntley!"

I stopped and turned. "Yes?"

"Do you need my mom to sign that progress report you gave me?" He pulled a slip of paper out of his back pocket, and with a wide smile suddenly filling his face, presented it to his mother. "Mom—look!"

She read the red-inked comments:

"Tony has a great personality and a wonderful sense of humor. When he uses them appropriately, both can be very helpful in a classroom. Please continue to encourage him to improve as a student."

After his mother had finished, Tony looked up at me. "Do you need this back?"

"No, that's for you to keep, Tony. I've got a copy. Hang onto it to remind you of what you are capable of." I smiled and left them waiting for the principal.

With Tony in Floresville, my class time became more productive. He was the number one consumer of my teaching time for 4 months. He was not a bully or a mean kid, just a big ego without any sense of consequences for his actions.

I wonder how there was room enough in my class for him and all the rest of us. I wonder how we survived him. I wonder why it is that I miss him?

Whack-a-Moles

Mornings are just a prelude, really. Everyone is sleepy in first period, drawn in dreamy wonder to their novels.

Second period I sit in the library, still a million miles from the brewing chaos. Team conference in third passes in a flash of idleness. I chat with Ms. Donahue and Ms. McCready over lunch, watching the clock and mentally preparing for my marathon afternoon.

It isn't even too tough in fourth period. Maybe it's the after-lunch daze, when all the blood is in their stomachs. In fifth period, I start to feel guilty, having so little planned for this day. But then it's passing period, and the incoming bodies blurring around me remind me what I have been waiting for.

"I don't want to be in Chapter 1! I'm going to sit up there with the regular class," Carmen shouts. Everyone in the room watches her storm up to the front and sit in a desk. Then they all look at me. On behalf of my student, I send them all an apologetic look, and then Sylvia and I continue with our respective lessons.

I look down. Only Moe is sitting in front of me, scowling. Where is everyone else? As if in answer, I hear the theme from the game, "Where in the World Is Carmen Sandiego?" and head over to the computer to try to take control.

Tony, Jose, Pepe, and Steven ignore my presence. I reach into the huddle and detach the mouse from the computer. "Aw, sir, give us back the 'rat,' " Pepe scolds me.

"C'mon, boys, I told you that we would use the computer later this week. Get back to your seats," I say, but there is no response. "Now."

I touch Pepe's shoulder, and he recoils from me, bolting across the room. He grabs two large pillows, each almost as big as he is, and hollers, "CAN I READ ON THE PILLOWS!??" I wince, but nod. He dives to the floor on top of them. Steven wanders toward the front of the room, looking around distractedly.

"Steven, please sit down."

"Huh?"

"Steven, come back here. You too, Pepe."

"Huh?"

"Steven and Pepe come here now." Suddenly, I have an idea. "Let's get you two started on a novel. A novel with a tape so you can listen and read at the same time."

Inside I try to plead the case that I am not bribing them, just surveying their learning styles. The prospect of playing with new toys has them helping me get tape recorders and headphones set up and audiotaped books chosen. Soon they are lost from the classroom behind the soundproof barrier of their large blue headphones.

At moments like this I feel like I am playing that Whack-a-Mole game you find at amusement parks, in which you bonk critters with a mallet as they pop up at random. I look around the back of the room. Four down, three to go.

Tony is still at the mouseless computer. He is scowling at the screen.

"Tony, it's not your turn to be on the computer today," I say. "You have a book to finish, so you can create your book-sharing project next week."

"You never let me play on the computer! I don't want to share no book project!" He slams his hand on the computer desktop and folds his arms. "I don't wanna do nothin' today." I fetch his novel, *King Kong,* for him. I place it in front of him silently and walk away.

Moe is still practicing his pout. I ask him what is the matter. "My eye hurts," he explains to me in great detail. He continues to scowl at the wall.

Jose sits staring intently at his pencil, which is lying in three broken pieces in his hand. Again, I suddenly have an idea. "Tony, you did a wonderful job helping Jose yesterday with his graph skills assignment. How would you two like to continue in the workbook? I think Jose would appreciate your help." Jose looks indifferently at his shattered pencil, but Tony perks up.

"I did good?"

"A great job."

After a pause, Tony says, "Okay, then, I'll help him. I won't give him the answers. Just help." Tony then heads to the desk where Jose sits. Somehow, I know I can trust them. Can't I?

I look over at Pepe, who is dashing my hopes again.

As Steven reads calmly and quietly beside him, Pepe is trying to make his headphones look like a football face mask. I ignore him when he looks up and calls out, trying to get my attention. Finally, he casts the headphones aside. "This is boring! I can't see words with those headphones on!"

I roll my eyes. I look in disbelief at the time. I want to check to see if the clock is broken.

Sixth period leaves me in a heap on a stool at the Chapter 1 table. Slowly, the seventh-period students gather around me. The look on my face must be pathetic. Eyebrows knit and faces close in to inspect my tattered remains. "Are you mad, sir?" Valerie asks cautiously.

"No, just tired," I say, smiling weakly.

Vanessa then saves my life. "Sir, can we read outside?" Eyes widen at the thought, waiting expectantly for my decision.

"What a wonderful idea," I reply.

We settle on the bridge by the north entrance. It is a beautiful day. Almost everyone spreads out to find a quiet place to read. I open Carlos's book for him, as he hangs like a chimpanzee from the bridge railing. To my surprise, he plops down next to me and begins to look at the pictures. It is a book about whales. Nice, large, slow-moving creatures.

I coax him to read aloud. I realize soon that three other students are hanging over our shoulders. " . . . 'And the blue whale can grow to 100 meters long.' How long is that, sir?" Carlos asks.

"About from here to that car over there."

"Wow, that's big."

"And look how big its heart is!"

" . . . 'As big as a small car'—really?"

"I guess so. Like that one." I point to Ms. Harper's Honda Civic.

We read together and explore the whales until it is time to go in. Things have come into focus again, moving at speeds I can handle. As we walk leisurely back to the room, the students rattle off several of the things they learned during our reading session.

And that is good enough for me.

Save the Children

The bell rang.

First period, as usual, was quiet and attentive. They squinted at the flag and murmured through nearly half of the Pledge of Allegiance. As the announcements chattered on, one of my students wandered into the room. I was about to scold her for being tardy, but in a moment changed my mind. "Good morning, Angelina," I said. "Please have a seat."

I did not see the frustration coming, although I should have. Angelina had been absent for over a week because of a suspension resulting from a long pattern of truancy during first period. Today, she was back, and was not happy to be there.

She retrieved her folder from the bin and pulled out the assignment I wanted her to do for catch-up. It was at that point that she seemed to make a decision. It is frustrating to come back to an overwhelming amount of makeup work. But I also knew that she came to me from a home life fraught with abuse and who knows what else. For whatever reason, she just stopped listening to me. She sat there, refusing to work. I came by every few minutes to prod her, but she would not get to work. I began to get frustrated.

Late in the period I came by, quite a bit firmer with my instructions. With that she threw down her folder, got up from her seat, and climbed into a desk next to one of her friends.

"Angelina, come here please," I said, calmly. Here we go again, I thought to myself.

I must have repeated the request a dozen times. She simply smiled and looked at her friends, or shot back a petulant "No." I realized that her friends and the rest of the class were now watching the confrontation, and my ego took over. "Angelina!" I yelled. She and her friends just giggled.

The bell rang, and she rose to leave. But boy oh boy, this was far from over. I chased her to the door. Breaking all the rules of classroom psychology, I blocked her exit and guided her back into the room. At this point, finally, I thought I saw her start to lose control. With a high-pitched, frustrated "No!" she stormed toward a seat, but the storm was over in a second. She crossed her arms, looked off to her left, and, by the time I was seated in front of her, was gone. Her body was sitting there, but Angelina was deep inside, behind a strong fortress wall.

I was not nearly that good. My heart was pounding, and my mouth was working a bit too fast for my common sense. And to tell the truth, I really wanted to get some reaction out of her. "Angelina," I began, "I want to know why you are treating me like shit!"

Oops. I don't think I really wanted to say that. But adrenaline pressed me onward, and I began a tight-jawed speech about respect and disappointment. As my lecture rambled on, I became conscious of the fact that my words were bouncing off her defenses and into oblivion. Even I was no longer listening to my voice, so I just stopped.

She was not going to come out to acknowledge me. Angelina was an expert at locking up her vulnerable self-identity to protect it from the verbal and physical abuse that it received at home, and even from an unthinking teacher at school. For a few moments, I studied her unblinking glare and noted a slight tremble in her lips. She heard me the second time I dismissed her, and stormed out of the room.

Fortunately, I had planning period next and was able to take a drive around the block to cool off. I sped around the neighborhood, screaming off my adrenaline rush. "I have to remember where she's coming from! I can't take it personally! I made the wrong choice!"

Hoping to verify my convictions that her behavior had a pattern and that it truly wasn't me she was reacting to, I watched her that day, in the halls, in line at lunch, and on her way out the door at 3:05. Her group of friends seemed to share her attitudes and personality traits, and from my experiences with them, I knew that at least some of them had similar situations at home.

There they were, clogging a doorway, whispering, glaring together at specific students they had it out for on that particular day. They packed together like a gang in the halls during passing period, wearing their fashion-fruity lipstick, their shiny, lacquered bangs, and their oversized sports team jackets. As a group, they manifested a frightening fortress from which they threatened those around them with the weapons of anguish, mistrust, and bitterness that boiled within.

Watching them burst into the front of the lunch line, I wondered what they all must have made of my confrontation with her, and what she had told them. "That Mr. Huntley—he can't do anything to us. If we stick together, that's all that counts."

In a way, she would have been right, I thought. What did behaving in school have to do with the anguish in their lives? To Angelina and her friends, school was a bunch of games for children. But I knew in my heart that a child hid within the defenses that Angelina constructed so well. That child belonged here in the sixth grade, where she could celebrate a few last innocent days before adolescence.

Embodied in the armored little girl named Angelina was a true example of someone at risk. She lived in a hard world where the child inside had to be concealed, stifled, even suffocated and forgotten if the human being was to endure. Angelina and her friends were covering the mouth of the crying baby, hoping the beasts would not find them, but unknowingly suffocating the child. I don't think they planned to destroy their innocent inner selves, but I saw Angelina near the end of the process of doing so.

I looked into the face of the girl as she walked past me, after school, headed for the bus. Was there someone left to save in there? And if so, what was left?

The next morning I saw Angelina with Christine, her cousin and a member of her pack. They were searching for the rest of their sisters-in-arms, decked out in their pouty bright lips and Aqua Net hairsprayed bangs. A teacher standing beside me also watched them wander down the hall, and broke our musing silence.

"You know, Angelina was an A student until about a year ago. She always helped Christine, who got Cs and Ds. Then she just stopped doing her work."

I watched the two join the coalescing pack at the water fountain. Angelina and Christine lived together with their grandmother. They shared the same home life, in which, as one counselor put it, many adults were all trying to wash their hands of them. I did not know much about Angelina, but Christine's mother was in a Kentucky prison, and her father had been shot by police. I knew that because Christine had told me. In fact, I had gotten to know her quite well from early in the year.

She had been switched from fifth period to fourth, to fit her into the Chapter 1 program. She had been just another loud, disruptive character in a mob of over 40. The first few days after the switch, she had sat silently in protest. As the days progressed, however, her eyes began to open wider, and she was looking around the smaller, quieter class with an awakened youthfulness.

It was during the most simple activities that I saw what had been unearthed in her. Sharing colors with two other girls, she pressed crayons white-knuckled to a scene from the journey of Christopher Columbus to the New World, visible to her through a skein of knotted black hair. Grinning contentedly, she sat snuggled in a corner of the room with another student, taking turns reading Shel Silverstein's poems aloud.

Unfortunately, I also saw the other side of her exposed childhood. When Christine was upset, it was time for a knock-down, drag-out tantrum. I once watched her squirm around on the floor for a good 5 minutes, tossing her folder's contents up into the air above her, shouting, "I HATE this class!"

To say the least, she had no problem expressing that kind of emotional immaturity. And to be honest, I had no problem with that. She was attempting to struggle with her anguish physically. I let her screech and stomp and flail, knowing that it would not last long. I ignored her when that happened, and reapproached her softly and gently when it was over.

It was somewhat strange to see such behavior in a girl who was clearly becoming physically more mature. Other teachers might have drawn the line much sooner, if only for the sake of the other students. But there was a struggle going on in her, a healthy conflict between physical maturation and a psychological contentment with childhood—the paradox of growing up.

I celebrated the fight left in Christine. But I feared that she was rapidly approaching a stage of development, much more related to her life and experiences than to physical changes, that would push her into the oblivion in which Angelina was floundering. During one 2-week period, she had run away from her grandmother to live with one of her many "aunts." She came to school unkempt, hair drooping, wearing an odd assemblage of clothes. She protested my presence with a grin and a calculated stare into the book in her lap. As I interacted with her, I tripped several times over the makings of a wall. But the structure was still thin, and did not repel me. With patience I had learned in my dealings with Angelina, I drew Christine back to her more familiar self.

After that episode, I again wondered: Can I reach a Christine or an Angelina once that wall has gone up?

The next day, as I had several times before, I forced myself to try to coax Angelina out of her defenses. I met with the same repelling "No," the same petulant "Go away!"

I pretended to need something in front of the room, so I could sweep by Angelina and see if it really was a note she was writing and not class work. Yes, it was. I tried humor. "I'll do that assignment for you. How much would you pay me?"

That day she actually began to talk to me, if only in an aloof manner, about one of my students who had been gone for weeks. "She's pregnant," she replied. "It was some high school boy."

The bell again interrupted our interaction. This time, I sadly wondered how much further we might have talked. But at the signal of freedom, she was up and gone, nearly running for the door.

"Angelina—" I called after her shrunken frame. "I'm so happy to see you enjoying reading class. See you tomorrow."

When I had gotten to "See you tomorrow," though, she was gone. Andy's face was peeking in the door at me. In a blur behind him, Angelina and two friends raced by to some prearranged rendezvous.

I'll start with the small things, I thought. Seeing her tomorrow. And the next day. If I can just preserve her as I found her last September, she might make it into a classroom that is, for her, secure. I have not given up hope if I can imagine that I kept her on the road toward a teacher she will listen to, a teacher who can save her.

A month later, Angelina and Christine withdrew from Mark Twain. It came as a surprise, after a rather pleasant team conference with Angelina. All the teachers took turns telling Angelina how much she had improved in the past 2 weeks.

But her stubborn neglect of self-responsibility dragged her down again. She refused to take off a jacket that displayed her gang's name on the back. She calmly defied all of her teachers, without provocation, without reason. In the seat before me, Angelina was wheeling, tumbling out of control. Benita went to get an administrator to take her away and confiscate her jacket. I was glad. I couldn't bear to see her hit bottom.

In the next few minutes the assistant principal came in and presented us with an option that had been on the back burner for some time. We consented unanimously to contact Angelina's guardian and have her withdrawn, deciding it was in her best interests to seek out a fresh start.

The end of my relationship with Angelina was fraught with unpoetic and cruel incidents. The first was the moment that Christine came in and announced that she, too, was withdrawing. The two stood with withdrawal forms urgently thrust at me. I floundered through my grade books and could not find the grades. I then sought out Benita, who had the grades, and caught up with the girls in Ms. Donahue's room. Along the way I wondered how this story might end. I even wondered if I could say something moving to seal this relationship right. But in the end, all I could manage was a "Goodbye and good luck," that they did not hear or chose not to acknowledge.

It really hurts when something so obsessive as this story must be cut away and stolen from me. As much as it was their right to be free of my invading concern, it was my right to be concerned. It is also my right never to forget them. To wonder if they are still alive in 5 years. To wonder if they ever will be saved.

Dirty Hands

It amazes me how dirty my hands get when I teach.

By fifth period every day, a second skin of chalk dust and school-lunch grease coats my palms and fingers. During sixth period, some ink from a broken pen and the saliva from its chewed cap add to the sheath of grunge. In seventh period, I pat a half-dozen sweaty shoulders just back from P.E. After school, I pry smashed chocolate candies off the floor and gather spitballs to throw away. On my way out the door, I stop to chat with a student carrying a damp, crumpled Kleenex tissue for his runny nose. Without thinking, I shake his hand to wish him a good afternoon.

Then, while driving home, I get the feeling. I reach up to scratch my head, and I suddenly feel the numbness. My hand is suffocating. I look at the hand paused in midair, blocking my view of the road, and I think I can actually see the stuff moving around on my skin. I cringe and twitch. My face wrinkles up. I am miserable for most of my ride home, overcome by the realization that my hands are completely, utterly, filthy.

When I get home, I frantically rush to the bathroom, turn on the tap with the tips of two grimy fingernails, pump two generous squirts of orange antibacterial soap into one hand with my elbow, and begin to scrub while sighing in ecstasy. Black gobs of soap bubbles fall into the sink, screaming for mercy as they slide down the drain. Ahh. Once again, my physical being is clean and pure and at peace with the world. My mind is ready for some nice, relaxing, idealistic reflection about what I believe in as a teacher.

In my anxiety, I experience the tension between the rolled-up-sleeves feeling of teaching in action and the higher philosophical aims I formulate about what I do. It's as if there are two opposing worlds for education, one seething with organic activity, the other a pristine latticework of ideas and beliefs. When I started my internship at Twain, experienced teachers laughed knowingly as I told them about the theories we were studying in our night classes. "All that philosophical thinking about education is interesting," they would say, "but you'll find it isn't worth squat in the classroom. That's teaching."

Meanwhile, in the seminar rooms at Trinity, I was being told to challenge that opinion. I needed to bring my philosophical beliefs into the classroom and act upon them as I taught. "That's professionalism," my professors said.

"Okay," I thought, smart-aleck just out of college and full of ideas. "I'll try it."

Very quickly I found out for myself that action and reflection in teaching can be worlds apart. The smell of a middle school, the whirlwind appearance of the classroom, the things there that have been touched, chewed, stepped on by adolescents—these things drive clean, well-crafted, long-prepared ideas from the building screaming in terror. Oh, you could probably heavily Scotch-Guard the ideals and smuggle them in, but don't expect miracles. "Be pessimistic," I hear teachers say in their hesitant suggestions about my grand ideas. "That way, you won't be disappointed when they don't work."

Do I dare put my emotional and intellectual foundations on the line every day by attempting to reflect on my deepest beliefs in the daily tempest of middle school? Is self-preservation a good enough excuse to answer, "No"?

I don't think I'm ready. I wonder if I will ever be ready. Every day, I drive home in my car, my hands feeling numb. I laugh at the notion that they get so dirty, I can't even feel anything with them. I hope it isn't the early symptom of something more dangerous, like a loss of faith.

But don't count me out yet. I still take great pleasure in returning to the safety of my home, where I can face the things I believe at the bottom of my heart. I wash my hands, and I tell myself, "I am a teacher." My ideals intact, my hands clean, I sit and reflect upon the day that, once the laughter and the tears have been wiped away, becomes a tool with which I may better myself. For now, it's the most professional thing I can do.

Why Can't I Be Their Friend?

One Friday in February, Samuel wandered in the room at 3:15.

"Sir, can I play with the computer?" he asked hopefully. I looked over at the Macintosh sitting idly in the back corner of the room. We had recently begun learning to use it in class, and there was a feverish excitement among students about the machine.

The idea was exciting to me as well. I was a card-carrying MacNerd. "Hey—yeah! Let me show you some of the things you haven't seen," I said, eagerly dropping my room-straightening chores for a bit of fun.

Samuel had already become adept with the mouse. He maneuvered us into *KidPix* without a hitch. He had been dying to try it out for several weeks. Pretty soon, we were exploring its broad dimensions of diversion. We sat together, taking turns trying different windows and buttons on the screen.

"Push that box—Oh! Ha ha ha!"

"Make it blow up the screen again!"

"Wow! How did we do that?"

"Hee hee," Samuel laughed through his toothy grin. "This is fun!"

Before we knew it, it was 4:15. We reluctantly shut down the machine and gathered our things.

Starting that day, Samuel and I were occasional afterschool play-mates. Equals as Mac lovers and funlovers. Except that I could drive and ended up driving him home.

Samuel sat like a well-worn rag-doll in my passenger seat, wearing the ever-present gray fleece pullover that looked like it had never been washed. His dark hair spiked and clumped in all different directions. He looked up at me, head tilted back and mouth slightly open. "Are you going out to party tonight, Mister?"

"Well, I'll probably go country-western dancing," I said, two-stepping around his implications of alcohol consumption. "So what do you do on the weekends?"

"I go to my friend Roger's to play Nintendo."

"Nintendo! I used to have one of those old Atari games. You know, the—" I paused, realizing that my Atari system was older than he was! I stepped outside myself and marveled at the situation: Here I am, shooting the breeze with a sixth grader. I spend my whole day teaching sixth graders, and then spend an additional hour with one. Am I crazy? Or just fighting hard not to grow up?

"Well, here's your street! I remembered this time!" I said, bringing the car to a stop right in front of his house.

"Check plus, Mister!" Samuel beamed at me, then opened the door. He climbed out carefully, then leaned in. "Bye bye!" Thanks shone in his contagious smile.

He carefully closed the door with both hands then ran to his front door. I slowly pulled a U-turn, gazing down the street of boarded-up, graffiti-covered houses. As I accelerated away, Samuel waved me off from behind his screen door. I waved back. I drove past a group of teens leaning on a chain-link fence. Samuel had pointed out his brother among the young men, all decked out in ensembles of black and brown, bandannas and stocking caps on their heads. When would they pull Samuel in, I wondered. Or was it already too late?

I avoided the troubling thoughts by remembering how much fun I'd had that day. I recalled my jokes with Samuel, jokes I wished I could share more often. With pangs of frustration and responsibility I was reminded of my teacher role: no favorites, positive adult role model, and don't get too close. Why couldn't I just be their friend?

FOUR

Mr. Henry

"To teach a kid well you have to know a kid well."

Ready or Not

I pushed my apartment door shut, let my books drop to the floor, and fell back onto the sofa. I looked at the refrigerator, but I was too exhausted and too discouraged to even think about putting a meal together. I would have turned on the TV and lost myself in one of those network shows, except that I didn't have a TV. So I sat and stared at the coffee table, where a TV would have been.

I felt utterly frustrated. My ideals were crashing. My lesson had gone badly, the kids had not learned anything, and Ms. Sanders had let me know it. I knew frustration hit every first-year teacher. Of course I would get frustrated with a student, with a lesson, or with a situation. But it was supposed to be manageable frustration. Not oppressive frustration.

I knew teaching would be hard. Especially at Mark Twain Middle School. I had never heard of anyone volunteering to do their internship at Twain. My roommate understood. He had decided to switch to elementary education after his experiences at Twain.

My own reaction to the news that I would be an intern at the middle school had been mixed. Like most of the secondary interns, I had originally requested to be placed at Lee High School. I was excited, however, when I learned that my mentor teacher at Twain would be Evelyn Sanders. I had worked with Ms. Sanders before as a practicum student, and I knew that I would learn a lot from her. I was excited by the challenge of teaching middle school. I believed that if I could teach inner-city eighth graders, I could teach anywhere.

Now, 2 months into my internship, I was doubting whether I could teach at all.

I was too quiet. I worked hard to get through the University speech requirement without having to take a public speaking course. I automatically subtracted the participation points in my college courses because I knew I would never speak up in class. I even hate birthdays because I don't like people looking at me while they sing. I dislike being the center of attention, yet I chose a profession in which I would stand up in front of 150 people a day.

I was too nice. I knew long before I stepped into the classroom that discipline would be one of the biggest challenges for me. I reflected back on the day. Third period always gave me the worst time.

"Edgar . . . Edgar! Please give María back her comb. Edgar . . . René, I need you to pay attention. Alex, you're going to need a piece of paper. Okay, listen up, what we're going to do is . . . Luis put that down! Mónica. Mónica! Leave those in the bookcase. What I want you to . . . Antonio where are you going?" When the period ended I sat and wrote in my journal.

> Why would anyone want to be a teacher? I don't want to be one! Not today. Stupid job. I just want to get on a bus and leave for Mexico. Monterrey maybe. Far away from people.

In the beginning of the year I was teaching three periods. Later on I would take over all five of them. Even with only three classes to teach I was exhausted and discouraged at the end of the day. I was supposed to teach kids, not fight them for their attention. I understood why so many first-year teachers quit.

"You've got to get them to respect you. You've got to develop your own sense of personal power," Evelyn kept saying. "It's not something I can teach you. I can show you what to do. I can model it. But I don't know, it's just something that's got to come from within you."

Ms. Sanders always had good advice for me. She was a tough lady with a North Texas accent who had been teaching for 23 years and wasn't about to let a 13-year-old drag her around the block. Kids sat up straight when she spoke to them. I sat up straight when she spoke to me.

"Even if you don't get mad you have to learn how to put on an act," she said. "That's all it is. It's not that I hate the kids. I really and truly don't, but you have got to let them know when they've crossed the line."

In spite of a good role model, I had thus far failed to develop that sense of power. No matter how I tried to look at the matter rationally, to put the feelings into context, and to remember stories of other successful teachers who had gone through their tough times, I still could not get over the feeling that I may really not be made out of whatever it takes to reach 13-year-olds.

I lay awake nights dreading the next school day. I did not fear the kids themselves. I never felt threatened; I liked them a lot. I did not worry that I was unprepared. What I feared was facing the class and being responsible for keeping control. I feared being in charge. I didn't want to be the authority.

I was not supposed to feel fear. People have called me a number of things in my life—quiet, shy, friendly, independent—but rarely timid. I spent one summer working 18-hour days in a fish cannery in Alaska; I was not afraid of working hard. Still I had a feeling I was up against one of the biggest challenges of my life.

I had conquered many challenges before. A letter on the coffee table from my friend Marius reminded me of the spring I traveled through Eastern Europe. "No one goes to Romania alone," I was told. "The living conditions are some of the worst in Europe, the new government is no different from the old Communist regime, and using public transportation is akin to 'being punished by God.'" I traveled to Romania alone anyway. I did not know what I was getting myself into, but I liked challenges.

Traveling in Romania was indeed difficult. A short train ride into the country turned into a many-hour-long ordeal as border guards searched through everything I owned. By the time I arrived in the town of Timisoara it was midnight, and I was in a strange place with nowhere to stay. Thankfully, a Romanian I had met on the train invited me to come along with him.

Marius, my Romanian friend, wrote to me.

"Don't forget! When you'll be in Europe don't avoid Romania, and when you are in Romania don't forget us. Anytime you'll be a dear guest for my family! Please do remember that."

Challenges, I remembered, aren't easy. They often aren't pleasant. They are, in the end, worthwhile.

A Prayer For Alex Garcia

Alex Garcia. Am I doomed to remember him forever? He was a part of my life for such a short period of time, and yet his memory remains fresh within me. It has refused to scar; rather it remains an open wound that has yet to heal.

"Alex! Back to your seat."

Time after time, I would guide this nice-looking youth back to his desk. Like a helium balloon in a gymnasium, he was always floating off to various spots in the room. More often than not, I retrieved him at the desk of his girlfriend, Marcela. I would sit him down and watch him take out a piece of paper. I would ask him if he had any questions about the class work, and he would shrug his shoulders and stare away blankly. He wasn't going to do any of it, and he and I both knew it.

"I don't care." About that, Alex was sincere. It didn't matter at all to him that in 10 weeks he had completed virtually no work in class. It didn't matter to him that he would not graduate to high school with his friends. He said he didn't care about his friends, or even about Marcela. About that, no one believed he was sincere.

"That's really nice looking." I complimented Alex on the picture of a rose he had drawn with Marcela's name written underneath. Gang signs adorned the outer edges of the paper. Alex really could draw beautifully.

"You do such good work. Why don't you take this assignment and do the illustrations? I'll give you a grade for it."

There was no response. I wanted him to talk to me. To let me know what he was feeling. To let me help him in some way.

I didn't know what to do. I had tried to talk with him privately. I had tried to talk with him in the hall. I had tried talking with him reasonably. I had tried being firm with him. It didn't matter what I said. He didn't listen. If he would not listen to me, at least I wanted to find a way to show him I cared. I tried a hand on the shoulder but he drew back immediately.

"I hate you." The boy, who would not give me a reaction, liked to try and get a reaction out of me. Determined to try to get something to grade out of him, I sent him to the Content Mastery (CM) room, where he could get more individual help. As I wrote out the pass I let me know what he thought of the CM room and of me. He thought all teachers were stupid. About that, he was sincere. He was angry, and he was hurting, and I didn't know what to do.

"What do you do when you're really angry?" Alex asked.

"Are you angry at someone or something, Alex?"

Alex didn't answer questions. If eyes are the windows to the soul, Alex had one-way glass. He could obviously see out. It was impossible to look in. It was impossible to see what inner struggles were hurting him so. It was impossible not to notice the outward clues.

During one class I was graphically depicting the number of casualties the Black Plague had taken, by pretending to kill off half of the class.

"You're dead René. Put your head down on your desk. You're dead Marcela. . . . You're dead Luis. . . ."

I continued around the room.

"Me, me!"

Begging to be killed was the most life in class I had seen out of Alex all week. Alex had real problems. He did not care about going to high school, he told us, because he really didn't expect to live that long.

"Alex's been suspended again." Mr. Sheberle announced the news at our team meeting.

There was not much to say. Alex's suspensions were becoming regular occurrences. Usually it was the result of a fight with another student. Alex himself knew that the fighting was going to have to stop. Too many suspensions and he would be transferred to another school. He did not want that to happen.

"What could another school give him that we haven't?" Shannon Walsh asked the question we all wondered. "We know him. We worked with him. Another school would just have to start all over at the beginning."

The beauty of working in teams is the ability to work together on students' problems. We had worked together with counselors. We had brainstormed ways to reach Alex. None of them had worked much.

Then one day Shannon came into team meeting excited.

"I think we've got it! Hats."

She had let Alex wear her goofy-looking straw hat, and Alex had finished half of his math problems. The next period Ms. Russel let him wear a hat in class and he had actually spent the time reading his book. How long such a gimmick would work we didn't know. For the moment Alex was working and he was enjoying himself. I determined to search my collection of odd caps for him to wear.

"Are you an M/C?" Alex asked another student.

The student stood up, afraid to acknowledge the gang and afraid not to, and Alex slugged him. He was out for another 3-day suspension. The next time he came to class it was with the long white carbon copy form asking for his grades. He was being withdrawn. I wanted to say something to him. I wanted him to leave knowing how much we cared. But he wasn't listening.

I don't know if the other school was able to do anything more for him. I doubt it. It hurts when I think about Alex. In my heart I hold onto the dream that, given more time, we could have reached him, that we could have helped him. Maybe we did in some way.

I hope so.

I don't come to school every morning to ensure that the future generation of Americans knows that Washington crossed the Delaware. I come because I want to help them. I come because I love them. If loving them means empowering them with knowledge and skills, then that is what I will do with my whole heart. In my heart I hold onto the dream that every student can be reached and that every student can be touched.

Dear Lord, I hope that someone, somewhere, will reach Alex. And that's about all I can do now: pray.

The Addiction

Okay, I admit it. I'm addicted.

How do you describe an addiction? I can't. All I know is that I've just got to do it. It doesn't matter what reasoning I use, what logic, what advice my mother gives me. Something within me just drives me forward.

"How do you like teaching?"

Doggone it, they always ask me that question. Friends from Trinity, friends from Montana, long-lost relatives, barbers, and taxi drivers. They always end up asking that dreaded question.

"If you can imagine something that every day makes you want to quit," I say, "that exhausts you and drives you to the verge of insanity, but you wouldn't want to be anywhere else in the world, that might describe it."

Or it might not. In fact, it rarely does. Only with other teachers do I get the idea that they have a notion of what I am trying to say. I feel powerless to make other uninitiated inquirers understand the incomprehensible.

I try to make others see the pains and joys of teaching. Either I get a nod, which indicates that they do not understand the number of teachers taking medication for ulcers and depression, or they say "How terrible, have you thought of trying another profession?"

Try something else? Does no one understand? It's an addiction. Of course I have thought about doing something else, but it shocks me every time I hear someone say it. Teaching is not terrible. It's great. I love it. It just feels terrible sometimes.

The root of the problem was exposed one particular day early in the semester. It was one of those sunny fall days in San Antonio that feels a lot like a sunny summer day in Montana. It was also during one of those days that I was doubting the reason for my existence.

Certainly my existence had not made much difference that day. At least that's how I felt.

It was 3:30 and I was glad to be free from the strain of teaching for another few hours. As I walked past the basketball courts back to my car, I noticed Carlos, Jorge, and Diego shooting around, apparently also enjoying their hours of freedom from school.

"Mr. Henry, you want to play with us?" Carlos asked.

As much as Texans love their football, Montanans love basketball. Addictions come in many forms, and I could not resist dropping my bags and heading over to the courts.

An hour later, hot and sweaty, and happy, I picked up my bags again.

"I have to go," I said. "I've got to grade all those papers you turned in."

"Okay, sir," they chorused. "See you tomorrow, Mr. Henry. You don't have to grade the papers, sir, you can just give us all 100%."

Before I got in my car I couldn't help turning around and watching them for a little longer. Something in their brown faces—which by age 14 had seen so much and yet so little of life—explained my addiction to teaching. Impossible as it is to describe, I knew why although I often fell asleep dreading standing in front of the class, I usually woke up anxious to get to school. It was to see them. To see Diego, Jorge, and Victor. To see Mónica, Miguel, and Claudia. To see Carlos, Eduardo, and Lucia. Yes, even to see David, Edgar, and Luis. To be a part of their lives. Maybe even to make a difference. Does that make sense?

Practice What You Preach

I'm so glad school is over. As soon as the kids clear the halls I'll be done. I just want to go home. How on earth is it possible that there are so many schools in the world—where do they find enough people willing to be teachers?

"What, Julio? No, I don't have a university class today or Adopt-a-Grandparent. . . . Well I was planning. . . . Well sure, why don't you meet me on the basketball courts in 10 minutes."

Jimminy Julio, why today? You're such a good kid, and you need so much attention. You love it when I stay and help you with your shooting. But I just want to go home and forget today. General George Melendez led second period in a coup attempt, and third period was the gauntlet again. Once I've gotten by Luis, René, Alex, and John, I still have Juan, Carlos, Edgar, Mónica, and Antonio waiting. By the time I get to the end of fifth period, I feel black and blue.

"How was school today, Julio? I guess that makes two of us who are glad it's over."

Julio used to be one of the major causes of school headaches. He was a constant disruption. I hated it when he ran his fingernails along the blackboard. He had a nasty attitude and a sneer that would have caused teachers to buy admission tickets to see him spanked. But since the time he found a girlfriend and we started playing basketball together, he has turned into one of the nicest kids. I guess he is receiving the attention he needs. He still needs to be reminded to stay on task. He becomes frustrated so easily because his reading level is so low, and he has such low self-esteem. But he isn't one of the problems in class anymore.

"Okay, let's see your shot, Julio. Just get your balance, concentrate, and stroke the ball through."

Raise your voice, they tell me. Stand up straight. Call on students by name. Project more energy. Okay Dr. Holtz, I've been doing all these things, but I still feel out of control. I still feel that I'm cheating them on their education because I'm not able to make them sit up and listen.

"That's okay, Julio. Here, try again. You'll get it. . . . Bring your elbow in and point it straight at the basket. I know it doesn't feel natural but you'll be a lot more accurate eventually. . . . Good shot! That looked really good. I know that one didn't go in, but keep shooting them the same way and they will."

"You've got to develop a voice," Evelyn keeps telling me. "Look at me," she says. "After all these years of teaching middle school they often have to tell me to quiet down." Great. Because however you develop a voice, I have yet to figure it out. I try hard, I really do. But right now, I just can't help thinking that I don't have whatever personality it takes to be in a classroom. If that's so, then I'm killing myself for nothing. I should just pack up and go back to Montana. Maybe I could get a job leading pack trips into the Bob Marshall Wilderness. At least they won't be using my staplers for ammunition.

"Julio, Julio! Don't get discouraged, they're not all going to go in. Who do you think you are, Michael Jordan already? It takes a lot of time and a lot of practice. Shooting a basketball isn't something you can just do. It's an art. You have to develop a feel for the basket, you have to develop touch. You'll get it. It just takes time."

The Metamorphosis

A few weeks ago, the rest of our team discovered what I had been trying to keep a secret.

"Could you raise your hands, Eric?" Mr. Sheberle requested.

Unthinkingly I did, and suddenly laughter burst out all around me like thunder in a surround-sound theater.

"Look! He's got ink on his hands," my fellow teachers roared.

"It's Alejandra!" they chorused, referring to a student with a particular knack for exploding pens on herself.

Embarrassed, I could do nothing but endure the mayhem. Because it was my first year of teaching and I was still relatively young, I had been trying to cultivate a mature, sophisticated manner. I don't know why, because none of my elder mentors was particularly mature or sophisticated, as was painfully obvious by the fun they were having at my expense. Nonetheless, I was trying to prove that I belonged in adult society. Now, however, I was caught blue-handed in the naked truth: I was becoming a 14-year-old.

The first clues of the metamorphosis appeared early in the year as I was collecting homework assignments. I suddenly felt a sharp sting in my fingertips. Without letting on to the class that there was anything amiss, I sneaked a look down at my hands. On the end of one finger, blood was slowly starting to ooze, and two red dots had appeared in the spot where I had inadvertently stapled my finger.

I wasn't worried. It could happen to anyone, I thought. Some people are just a little more accident prone, I said after the second time.

I began to realize the situation was becoming more serious. My good friend Stacy and I were planning a little celebration in honor of her passing the entrance examinations to medical school (where you are never allowed to staple your fingers).

"How about if we go skating?" I suggested.

"Skating? I haven't been skating since I was in junior high."

"Neither have I," I answered. "It just sounds like fun."

I soon fell into the great junior high addiction: chewing gum. Never before having seen a need to eat anything you can't swallow— I hope all those bobbing Adam's apples when I call a gum check in class aren't what I think—but I was soon up to two packs a week. I did, however, remember to keep my mouth closed while chewing. Apparently the regression wasn't complete.

I began to become very self-conscious. I avoided eating any candy that would turn my mouth blue, and was sure never to make strange anatomical noises in public. But I was torn in an inner struggle between the responsible adult world and a strong desire to put a "Kick Me" sign on Dr. Holtz's back.

It was late in the first semester during our class at Trinity when I made a remarkable discovery of my own. We were discussing important and lofty educational theory on the use of metaphor in the pedagogic setting, and like an Old West false hotel front (proving how much attention I was paying to metaphors), I sat working to maintain the façade of academia. Then it happened. Dr. Holtz asked us to take out a piece of paper.

"Just a piece or a whole sheet?" Jeff asked, trying to keep a smile off his face.

Someone else had been afflicted as well! I almost fell on the floor. Luckily I had been coaching many of my students just a few weeks before in how to balance in their seats without falling off and was able to avoid an embarrassing moment.

"A whole sheet." Dr. Holtz looked perplexed at the question.

"Are we going to get a grade on this?" Jeannette asked.

"Can we do it for homework?" asked Shannon.

"Can I go to the bathroom?" asked Jennifer.

"Sir! This is too hard!" whined Laura.

It wasn't just me! I suddenly felt a release.

"Sir, Heather's poking me!" I couldn't help but join in.

From then on I felt no shame. To teach a kid well you have to know a kid well. Wasn't that what they were teaching us? And how can you really know a junior-high mind unless you can think with one? I realized that once I allowed the metamorphosis to take place, I began to understand what I was really doing in the classroom. I started to see through my kids' eyes. I began to see which of my activities were "boring," which ones they wouldn't understand, and even which ones they might really learn from.

I now see that teaching middle school takes a special breed of teachers who understand the unique abilities and inabilities endowed solely on those undergoing their own metamorphosis into teenagers.

A Smile a Day
Keeps Summer School Away

✳

Sandra had the sweetest smile. No matter what was on her mind she always seemed to be able to come out with a face that reflected the beautiful side of life. Not that Sandra was a model student. During the first 6-week term she did poorly in nearly all of her classes, and was well below passing in my own. As with many of the students, her problem was not a lack of ability but a lack of responsibility and motivation for doing her homework. Nor was she a model of perfect behavior. Her nonstop talking and defiant behavior had earned her numerous after-school detentions and chats in the hall with her teachers.

At the beginning of the next 6-week term I saw Sandra walking down the hallway. Everyone else was in class. I called her over in my most commanding teaching voice and proceeded to tell her that I really enjoyed her smile, and that it made me happier everyday when I saw it. She smiled even bigger, in a way that only an eighth grader who has had something good said about her or him can do, and went on her way.

As the term progressed she began to turn in a greater percentage of her work. In particular she seemed to be keeping up her folder well. It was not the best folder. There are some very gifted students in the class. But there were many others who had not even begun to organize one at the time. So, after asking Sandra for permission, I held up her notebook for the class as an example of how a folder should look. She beamed, proud of her work.

Her behavior during the 6 weeks improved as well. She is a girl who will always be talkative, but she became much more sensitive as to when it was appropriate to talk. By the end of the 6 weeks she was asking for her late work to make up, which she did well—unusual for students who turn in late work only to get it done. By the end of the 6 weeks she had raised her grade from an F in the first term to an A.

Unfortunately, Sandra's success was not in all areas. In some classes she did well and her behavior was fine, but in others she still was not putting in the effort and her behavior continued to be intolerable.

I would be naive to believe that Sandra's turnaround in her history class came directly as a result of my complimenting her. Yet within those compliments on her smile and her folder were messages that said "I like you," "You're special," and "You're a good student." These, I believe, became valuable to her. They helped create a relationship between us that was based not on my position as teacher and authority, but rather on a special understanding between us that she felt compelled to live up to.

I think this relationship between teachers and students is becoming one of the most important aspects of teaching. If there is going to be actual learning, there must be active involvement on the part of the student. And if someone is going to learn, whether the person is 13 or 30, he or she must have a reason for doing so. These reasons can come from a number of places; it may be that the subject itself is interesting to the person, or that he or she really does see the importance of learning it. In the past it has often been cultural or parental expectations. But in modern America many of these aspects are gone, and the only motivating force left is the teachers themselves.

Good teachers have always been known to compliment their students. But in a world of broken homes and violence, the encouragement of their teachers may be the only thing students can hold onto that makes them feel good about themselves.

I hope that Sandra and I taught each other a lesson. I hope that I taught her not only some history but also that she really could be successful if she wanted to be. I know she taught me the power of finding that special attribute in students with which to strengthen their sense of self-worth and confidence, and create a bond of solidarity that is so necessary in teaching today.

And I still remember the day clearly, when, years ago, my teacher Miss High complimented my smile.

Give It Your Best Shot

"Vanessa!"

Coach Wilson was off the bench and yelling as Vanessa dribbled the ball off her leg out of bounds—a turnover we didn't need. The game was close and tensions were high. Middle school girls' basketball can be just as exciting as the NBA at times, and the players and parents often take it just as seriously.

"They're trying to start something," Evelyn complained when the girls huddled for a time-out. All of the girls were playing with a high level of intensity, and the play was rough at times. From the bench, as the assistant coach, I kept an especially close eye on Vanessa. We were playing Kennedy, a team of big Black girls from the East side, and as one of the few Black students in our primarily Hispanic school, Vanessa was showing a particular pressure to prove herself.

As the girls headed back for their benches, one of the opposing players gave Vanessa a shove. Instantly I was out on the court as an adolescent riot erupted around me. I grabbed Vanessa and dragged her back to our bench. She struggled like a cat in a bath trying for a shot at the girl who had pushed her. I never saw the fists or the fighting, so intent was I on keeping a hold on Vanessa, but both Ana and Emily came away with bruises. The whole scene was ugly, even after the other team drove their bus away.

"You can't just go after another player," I warned Vanessa. "You not only could get yourself in trouble, you could get our whole team in trouble. You have to be tough enough to walk away from those situations."

"My mama told me that if anyone hit me, I could hit them back."

How can I teach them that violence is not an answer in life when fighting is the acknowledged way to gain respect in the world they live in? How can I teach them that violence leads nowhere when Marco, usually the loner, comes back from a 3-day suspension for fighting and suddenly other students are crowding around him in admiration?

Students complain that studying history is all about dead people and has nothing to do with real life. How much more real could we get? We had just finished studying the Boston Massacre. I don't really expect them to remember the year it happened. I wouldn't even mind if they forgot about Samuel Adams. We tried to answer the questions that the people involved would have had to ask themselves—when is it justifiable to use violence? I don't believe there is a right or wrong answer. As I often did, I had the students write their own responses to the question. I wanted them to probe their own lives and feelings, to interact with the ideas. Nearly every student wrote that violence was not a good solution because it leads only to more violence. I believe they meant it. But if what they learn doesn't *change* them, then what kind of learning is it?

The third fight of the week started when Silvia hit Paoula with the door on the way into class. They were instantly in each other's faces.

"Paoula!" I tried to get her to focus her attention on me.

"Let it go, don't get yourself in trouble over nothing."

"What happens if we fight?" she asked.

"It's an automatic 3-day suspension. Just cool off and forget her."

Paoula did cool herself next door in Ms. Walsh's room, but she didn't forget. It wasn't 5 minutes into the next day's class that I had both of them down in the office for throwing punches at each other.

Many times real learning does not come from the curriculum at all. Earlier in the week our point guard María had trouble brewing with another girl on the team. María was aggressive on the court and off.

"If you get in a fight, I don't know if Mr. Henry or I would ever talk to you again," Miss Walsh warned her. We knew, and she knew, that even if she was thrown into Juvenile Hall, we would still be there for her, but she understood.

And more important, she listened. When the fight with the Kennedy basketball team erupted, María was the one player who kept herself out of the fray.

"You taught me about the game of basketball," she told me later. "But more important you taught me about the game of life. I don't know what road I would have taken if it wasn't for you and Ms. Walsh."

Questions and Answers

How Has Violence Affected Your Life?

I do have a fear of crime, especially guns. Almost every night I hear gun shots, especially on weekends. Even my grandma is scared to come to our house, because last time she was here some guys started shooting at this man and his wife and baby. All three of them came up on our porch, and he started shooting back. They were hitting our house with bullets and there were six kids inside. The lady started ringing our doorbell to watch her baby so we did and called the police. Since then I have been scared of shootings.
—Daniela Villegas

The impact of crime has really turned my life around, not only on how late I stay out, but other things too.

At school I'm always worried about gangs or if someone will jump me for a certain color of clothing I am wearing.

At night I lay in bed listening to all the sirens and yelling. It kind of scares me sometimes, because I hope it's not happening at my dad's bar, which is next-door to my house.

Sometimes I have nightmares that someone has done something to my family. Someone has just got to stop all this crime, because it is not fair to anyone.
—Christine Smith

How I Feel About HIV/AIDS

All I know is that I'll try to be safe because I don't want any bad diseases in my body. I don't even think I'm ready to sleep with my boyfriend, because he already asked me, but he's been to bed with *a lot* of different girls. And I don't know if anything is wrong with that or what. And I really do love him and he tells me he loves me too, but I don't know what to do.

—Sandra Garcia

What Is the Culture at Mark Twain?

To explain this you have to know what a culture is, which is the way of life of a group of people, how they act, that sort of thing.

Going to school here at Mark Twain is kind of fun. The people here look mean at first, but when you get to know them they're okay. Some people just look at you and just say that they don't like you and they don't even know how you act around people.

—Shelita Johnson

The reason I do not like this school is because all our teachers are white, and there are two kinds of gangs. There should only be one kind.

—Magda Rodriguez

Mark Twain Middle School is one of the best schools in San Antonio. You are a very lucky person if you get the privilege of attending Twain. I should know. I go there.

Twain usually has a very loud and happy environment. Some kids do small things while others do more serious things.

One of the things at Twain that makes it different is that it is one of the few schools that has teams. In a team, students and the teachers get closer together. In general, the teachers are pretty good. Some of them are better than others, but none of them are perfect . . . and none of us is perfect.

One more thing, the worst teachers are from Montana. (Just kidding, Mr. Henry!)

—María Garcia

My Personal Identity

My characteristics have changed by meeting new friends, and talking with them. I concentrate more on my work this

year than I did last year, because I want to make my parents proud. I am more talkative this year.
—Guiliana Gálvez

I think I am not the same as last year because I was a lot meaner last year. Also I'm probably more into school this year, as I could prove with report cards.

I am starting to like to read and write more and so I am changing a lot this year.
—Pietro Alvarado

Well, first of all, I have changed a lot and for a lot of reasons. One may be that my dad took off. Which is really nothing big because he was always gone. He just came to visit and leave. Another is my mom. She always puts pressure on me that I'm the man of the house and I have to take care of my brother and sister. Another reason I changed is when they shot me. Believe me, it's a whole new level.
—Mario Lopez

In the Eye

*To teach a kid well you have to know a kid well. You
don't want to live in the same neighborhood. To
influence a kid you have to know a kid well.
You don't want them to see you in your sweats.*

*True teaching occurs after class, in the hallways,
on the playground. Maintain your role as a
teacher. Informal activities are essential
for building trust and confidence. Don't
be too chummy with the students.*

*Teachers have to be parents as
well. Never touch students. Nearly
every student struggles with
poor self-esteem. Don't tell
students you love them.*

*You can't wear your heart
on your sleeve. We need
to be open and honest
with each other.
We all gotta die
sometime sir.
I hurt. I'm dirt.
You need to
keep your
professional
distance.*

*Hot air going one way.
Cold the other.
It causes a
tornado of
voices
And I stand
in the eye
Wondering
where
to move.*

Basketball and
the Art of Classroom Maintenance

"You better be ready, Mr. Henry. I've been practicing."

"I'm ready. You just name the time and the place."

"That's good, 'cause you know the rookie is gonna take you to town this time."

"Sorry son, but your time has not yet come."

"We'll just have to see 'bout that. I've been practicing."

Antonio hurried off to his next period class. A smile lingered on both of our faces. Talking some trash in the hallways was a morning ritual for us. We had a best of seven basketball series going, and once every couple of weeks we would meet after school for the next round.

I never could be quite sure what was going on in Antonio's head, but I loved him anyway. This was his first year in regular classes after being in the Behavior Improvement Program. He always has to be moving to speak. Of course, he has to be moving to do anything else as well. Those who teach him agree that what he really needs is a seat belt. He cannot sit still. At any time he will be out of his seat and wandering around the classroom. He is not unintelligent, but his grades are low because he cannot concentrate on a subject long enough to master it. Inattention leads to distraction, distraction to disruption.

At the beginning of the year Antonio was nothing more than another lethal cannon in a third-period class created to shoot down upcoming teachers. He had failing grades, and his behavior was threatening his placement in regular classes.

Later in the year, as I grew more comfortable with teaching, I was able to reach out to more students individually. Antonio was one of them, and it paid off. Slowly his grades began to improve. He needed constant attention. A mentor from a San Antonio college was found to sit with him during class once a week. Often he was able to get his work finished in the Content Mastery room. He was always required to show me his progress reports as soon as he got them.

One day near the end of the year, he came up to me before school. "You beat Edgar?"

I nodded.

"I wanna take you on," he proclaimed, arms emphasizing the challenge. "And," he never could say anything without embellishing it, "the winner gets a pack of M-&-Ms."

The next day he presented me with the winner's purse.

"I'm not done," he said. "No no. We got to play a series. You just won the first game. Next time, it's going to be a different story." He went on embellishing for another couple of minutes before the bell rang.

And so began our series.

What is the role of a teacher? Is it merely to teach students? Antonio and I have worked together in the classroom and on the basketball court.

"I'm not gonna flunk," he stated one day in the hallway in the same matter-of-fact tone that he used to announce our games.

"Of course not," I said. "You're unstoppable. You may get beat a few times along the way, but when you put your mind to it, there's nothing that's going to stop you."

"That's right. I'm unstoppable. I'm the Shaquille O'Neal of my day."

Antonio made up all of his missed work and earned an A.

In the classroom, I am his teacher. I have no trouble being firm with him. In the halls, I am his mentor. I want to know how he is doing in his other classes. After school, I am his big brother.

However you define it, we have developed a relationship during the course of the year— a relationship that I have with each of the students.

Now I am about to learn what may be one of the hardest lessons in teaching. How to leave.

How do you spend a year working with someone, getting to know him on his good days and bad, watching his joys and hurts, his victories and losses, and then walk away at the end? Where does your heart go?

Can I Care Too Much?

I see them every day,
I see the look,
The eyes that say
I hurt so much.

I don't know what to do,
I see the look
And I hurt too.
Can I care too much?

When they talk to me
I listen,
Trying not to see
There's nothing I can do.

Families and fights,
The sound of guns
Ringing in the night,
I can't come to the rescue.

Sometimes they say
It would be easier
If we would go away
Not care; leave them alone.

How can I teach,
How can I
Really reach
Them if I can't take them home?

What they need to live
Is it possible
To give,

A simple caring touch?

Can I give my heart away
Without expecting
It back some day?
Can I care too much?

Should I even try?
Or would it
Be a lie,
If they believe my heart
Is far apart
From their fragile lives?

The End

I can't believe it's over. No, I really can't believe it. It hasn't really sunk in that this was the last day. This all-encompassing, life-changing, life-threatening experience is over.

I didn't teach today. I couldn't. We just turned on the radio and talked. Ms. Sanders presented me with the cartoon book *School Is Hell* and all the students signed it in appropriate places.

Mario didn't come; neither did Mónica. I didn't think Mario would, even though Ms. Walsh and I made his younger brother take a note home asking him to please come for our last day. I don't know where he is. He hasn't been in school for 3 weeks. Mario doesn't skip school just for fun. I hope he's in Juvenile Hall. At least there he's safe.

I knew Mónica wouldn't come. She had been in the Alternative Center for coming to school stoned and then had run away from home. The last time I saw her, the expression on her face was vacant. She had given up. There was no fight left in her.

After school today, Ms. Walsh and I met for one more basketball game. Antonio had already gone home, but Julio was there, and Diego, Carlos, Ana, Emily, and John. After a year spent getting to know students, and using basketball as a means to do it, it made for a nice closure.

"Look, Sir," Julio told me. "I can shoot now."

Indeed he could. I wanted to say, Look, Julio, I can teach now.

Leaving is the problem. How to leave Julio, and Diego, and Carlos. I like teaching. I still have my rough days in front of the class. My students still tell me I'm a little too nice (but not all the time). I am confident in what I'm doing. I am a teacher.

I still don't know what I'll do next year. Maybe I'll teach in San Antonio. Maybe in Montana or Alaska. Or maybe I'll teach English in Eastern Europe. Wherever I go, this year will go with me. I can only hope that this year at Twain has changed my students as much as it has changed me.

When we finished the basketball game, and the students were walking away, John reached out for a final handshake. John, the gang member who could always be trusted to have a graffiti marker in his possession. It's the first time I connected with him all year. The stories go on, but I won't be there to help write them.

Epilogue

Silence is a rare noise at Mark Twain.

Laura: It almost doesn't seem fair that we were able to put our stories together and call it our "portfolio." It's hard for me to even call it that. It seems to have more life—more energy—running through it.

Corinne: Except that we're growing, and it's static.

Jeff: But don't you feel that the stories have taken on different meanings, alternative significances, in our 2 years of experience since?

Laura: Yeah. It's a good sign that our stories might be of value to other teachers or intern teachers.

Jeff: Or people considering taking the plunge.

Corinne: For me, the stories were the best picture of my year I could imagine. Not like a diary, but as an artistic impression of the experience.

Laura: After writing the stories, we didn't need to show examples of our lessons, what worked and what didn't.

Jeff: Or have photos of projects—

Corinne: Or some abstract with concise summaries of our objectives and the outcomes.

Laura: And our stories paint an even more important picture when you stick them together. They show our concern for peer support, professional teamwork, and, above all, the kids we taught.

Jeff: But why are we trying to justify all of this to each other? We need to get working on our Preface!